THE BACKYARD
ASTRONOMER

FRANKLIN WATTS, INC.
NEW YORK, 1973

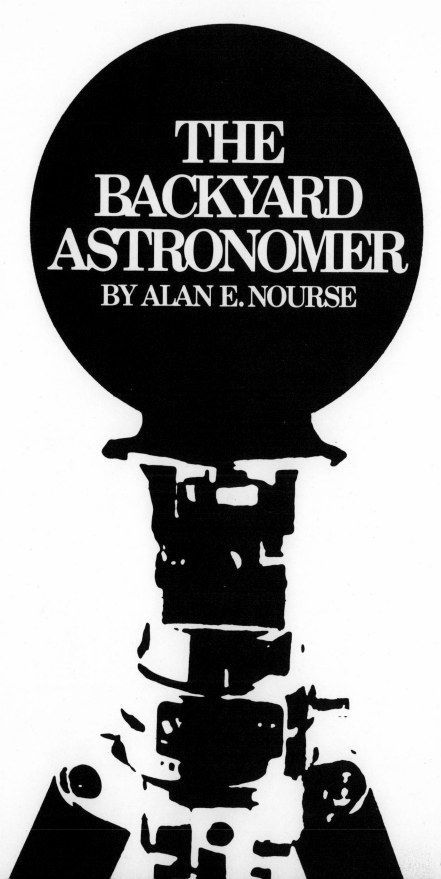

THE
BACKYARD
ASTRONOMER
BY ALAN E. NOURSE

Cover design by One + One Studio
Diagrams by Vantage Art, Inc.

Library of Congress Cataloging in Publication Data

Nourse, Alan Edward.
    The backyard astronomer.

    1. Astronomy–Observers' manuals. I. Title.
QB64.N68   523   73-4644

ISBN 0-531-02568-3

CONTENTS

THE BACKYARD
ASTRONOMER

1

THE INCREDIBLE SKY

Have you ever looked up at the breathtaking splendor of a brilliant starry sky at night? Of course you have. Everyone knows what the nighttime sky looks like. But how much of that sky have you ever really seen, and how much have you been missing all this time? For a surprising answer, try a simple ten-minute experiment the next evening the stars are out. It could open your eyes to a whole new and exciting world of adventure in your own backyard.

Pick a clear, cold, moonless winter night, or a sparkling midsummer evening well after the last trace of sunlight has faded. Then go outside to an open area away from lights or obscuring trees. All you will need is an ordinary kitchen timer and a good pair of binoculars. First, before your eyes are accustomed to the dark, look up at the sky just as you have a thousand times before. You will see stars, some bright, some dim — the same stars you have always seen. Perhaps you will recognize one or two constellations — the Big Dipper, low in the sky to the northwest, or possibly Orion, the giant Hunter, striding across the winter sky.

(Actually, the Big Dipper is an *asterism*, meaning a group of stars within another constellation; in this case, Ursa Major.)

You may also notice the hazy, luminous band of the Milky Way streaming across the sky from one side to the other. What you are seeing is probably as much as most people ever really see of the nighttime sky, glancing up briefly as they hurry from one place to another: a sky with some stars in it, and nothing more.

Now sit down for a moment, set the timer for ten minutes, and close your eyes. Keep them closed until the timer goes off. Don't peek; use your hand or a blindfold if you have to, bearing in mind that ten minutes will seem like a very long time. Then when the timer goes off, open your eyes and look again at that dark and starry sky.

What you see now may surprise you. Where there were a few dim stars before, now there will be hundreds filling the sky from horizon to horizon. The bright stars will be far more luminous now, and you will see myriads of stars that you couldn't see at all before. Even the familiar constellations will seem to be filled with stars that you would never ordinarily notice. What is more, you will see that many of the stars have very distinctive colors. Some will appear an orange-red, some bright scarlet. Some will look sapphire blue, others distinctly yellow, white, or even greenish in hue. Even more remarkable, what you saw before as a mere band of hazy light across the sky — the Milky Way — now will appear much brighter and more distinct, with definite edges, like a river of light made up of multitudes and swarms of tiny, close-packed stars — more stars than in all the rest of the heavens put together.

Finally, look at the Milky Way through the binoculars. If you thought you saw many stars with the unaided eye, you will be amazed at the dazzling multitude that will appear in the glasses, stars so numerous that it staggers the imagination. Then shift the binoculars to other more "empty" areas of the sky. Empty no more! Here, too, hundreds of stars that you could barely see at all before will spring into view, standing out like sparkling jewels against a black velvet background, brilliant pinpoints of red, blue, yellow, or white light. The more you look, the more you will see. And if you are stirred by awe or amazement or fascination at that crowded, starry firmament you may really be *seeing* for the first time, you are merely sharing the same sense of wonder that has stirred human imagination since time immemorial. This same vast starry sky has entranced stargazers throughout all history and has led to a scientific study of the heavens that is still opening up the secrets of the universe to this very day, the science of astronomy.

And if this ten-minute experiment makes you want to see and learn more, to explore a little further, you will be joining a vast brotherhood of amateur astronomers throughout the world who share together one of the most exciting and fascinating of all hobbies: a pleasant, informal study of the nighttime sky that we might speak of as "backyard astronomy."

But how can a backyard stargazer call himself an "astronomer"? Everyone knows that real astronomers are highly trained scientists who work in professional observatories using multimillion-dollar telescopes and other complex instruments. What can an amateur learn about the universe of planets, stars, and galaxies without years of study and access to professional equipment? The surprising truth is that you can learn an enormous amount about the fascinating world of astronomy quickly and easily from your own backyard — and have a thoroughly exciting time doing it. It is remarkably easy to learn when to look at the night sky under what viewing conditions in order to discover for yourself multitudes of celestial objects you may only have read about in books. Many of these objects can be located and observed with no other equipment than your own unaided eyes. Many other heavenly objects and displays can be studied even better with the aid of a good pair of household binoculars, especially if you can build a simple support to help you hold the glasses steady.

For other observational targets you will need a telescope — but not necessarily a large, powerful instrument requiring a major investment. The telescope used by the great Italian scientist Galileo when he discovered the four largest satellites, or moons, of Jupiter was hardly more complicated than the sort of simple spyglass that is sold today as a children's toy. The amateur astronomer today can find years of excitement and pleasure searching the sky with a small backyard telescope that need cost no more than a 10-speed bicycle or a good stereo set.

Even a fine telescope may prove disappointing or frustrating, however, until you have gained a certain amount of basic background knowledge about what sort of objects to look for where and under what conditions.

● *Conditions for Observing*
While it is possible to view the stars on some occasions from practically anyplace on earth, viewing conditions are far better in certain areas and at certain times than at others.

What things interfere with good astronomical viewing? Sky glow, clouds, and smog are the major offenders. If you could do all your observing from an artificial satellite in orbit out beyond Earth's atmosphere at times when both Sun and moon were hidden by the Earth's shadow, you would always have ideal viewing conditions. All the stars would then appear crystal bright and brilliant against the black background of space. But when you look at the sky from your own backyard or rooftop, you are peering through a thick blanket of air which is often filled with dust, moisture droplets, and other pollutants. If you live in the country, you will have fewer problems than the city dweller; clouds, of course, may interfere, but on clear evenings there will be no sky glow from city lights, and the country air will be comparatively clean and free of smog.

The best conditions for observing, then, are found in rural areas during periods of clear, dry weather well after the last glow of sunlight has faded from the sky. In northern latitudes, winter nights may be better than summer because much of the moisture in the air is frozen and precipitated from the atmosphere; the winter sky often appears particularly dazzling. Winter nights are longer, too, providing more time for observation, but they are also much colder. Summertime viewing will be more comfortable, and conditions can be splendid when the weather is dry, even though you have fewer hours in which to work. Bright moonlight can be a bother in any season unless, of course, it is the moon you want to observe. Otherwise you may do best to avoid moonlit nights, or to wait until there is a new moon or only a small crescent in the sky.

What about the city dweller? Downtown city sky glow can interfere seriously with star watching. In many residential or suburban areas, however, this illumination will be subdued in the late evening so that observing will be possible from a backyard or rooftop away from house lights and streetlamps. As for dust, smoke, or auto fumes in the air, the smog level in most cities varies with the weather. A thunderstorm or an offshore breeze can sweep away even a dense smog layer in a few hours and leave the air bright and clear for observing the next evening. You may also be able to plan periodic excursions out of the city, or to mountain or desert areas, where conditions for viewing will be much improved. But even in the heart of the biggest city, adequate viewing conditions can be found at least part of the time; the city dweller need only be alert for the dark, smog-free evening and seize the opportunity when it arises.

● *Adapting Your Eyes*
Wherever you live, and whatever the conditions for viewing, you will always be able to see far more if you allow time for your eyes to adapt to the dark before you begin viewing, and then take care to maintain your dark adaptation until your viewing session is over. Although man is not normally a night-seeing creature, his eyes can become accustomed to conditions of dim light very quickly.

The human eye is equipped with a circular diaphragm known as the *iris* — the colored part of the eye — which works much like the diaphragm of a camera. When light strikes the eye under normal daylight conditions, tiny muscles cause the iris to contract, limiting the amount of light that can enter the eye. But in dim light these same muscles relax, allowing the *pupil* — the "black spot" in the center of the iris — to dilate and admit as much light as possible. This process of pupil dilation, which requires several minutes to reach its maximum, permits a marked improvement in vision under dim light conditions.

To the backyard astronomer this simply means that he will be able to see far more in the sky if he allows his eyes to adapt to darkness before he begins his viewing than if he walks out of a brightly lit room and stares up at the sky immediately. The simplest way to dark-adapt your eyes is to follow the procedure described at the beginning of this chapter. Go outdoors in the evening and cover your eyes for a period of ten minutes or so. At the end of that time you will not only see more stars more clearly, but you also will be able to perceive varying shades of star color far more readily. Unfortunately, however, you will lose your dark adaptation very quickly if your eyes are exposed to white light even for a brief moment once they are dark-adapted. Try to avoid going in and out of doors during a viewing session and keep your eyes away from house lights and streetlamps.

If you must use a flashlight to consult a star map or adjust your binoculars or telescope, wrap the lighted end in advance with two or three layers of red cellophane that you can purchase at any ten-cent store or art supply shop; red light does not destroy dark adaptation and cause the iris to contract the way white light does. Some amateur astronomers even use red goggles to help maintain their dark adaptation during viewing sessions, especially when there is a bright moon in the sky. These can easily be made by knocking the smoked lenses out of a cheap pair of sunglasses and covering the frames with red cellophane. The glasses can be kept handy for use when a light must be used, but should of course be removed for your observation. With a little practice you will soon learn to maintain your dark adaptation even throughout prolonged viewing sessions.

● *The Space Around Us*
To the beginning backyard astronomer first stepping outdoors on a clear, dark night, it may seem that the sky is filled with stars, each one much the same as all the rest. It is only when you have become familiar with certain key stars and constellations, certain "guideposts in the sky," that you will begin to make sense of the confusing pattern of stars and be able to single out a particular celestial object from all the rest when you want to. Familiarity with the star patterns is such an all-important first step to enjoyable backyard stargazing that we will devote the whole next chapter to some simple ways that the beginner can orient himself. But first we must review what we know about the space immediately around us — the position of our planet Earth and the solar system in relation to the multitudes of stars that are visible in the nighttime sky.

First, we know that the Earth is one of nine planets traveling as natural satellites in orbit around a medium-sized, yellow-white star, the Sun. Like all the other planetary orbits, Earth's path around the Sun is almost but not quite circular; it forms a slightly elongated circle known as an *ellipse* around the Sun, and one complete circuit of the Earth in that orbit takes approximately 365¼ days. The orbits of most of the other planets lie in much the same plane around the Sun as the Earth's orbit does (see Fig. 1), so that if we could move a long distance outside the solar system and look at it edge on, it would resemble a flat disk with the Sun at the center. The plane of the Earth's orbit around the Sun is known as the *ecliptic*, and the orbits of the other planets vary only a few degrees from this plane with the single exception of the strange planet Pluto, whose orbit is tilted slightly more than 17 degrees from the plane of the Earth's orbit.

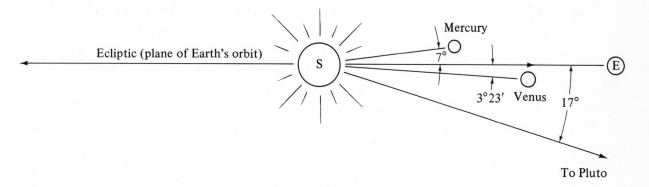

Fig. 1: Plane of the ecliptic and planetary inclinations.

The Sun, Earth's own moon, and the other planets of the solar system are the closest of all the heavenly bodies to the Earth — closer by far than the nearest star, but not all the planets are easily distinguishable. They shine only by light reflected from the Sun; the outer planets Uranus, Neptune, and Pluto are so distant from the Earth that special observatory instruments must be used to find them. Only the five planets closest to the Earth — Mercury, Venus, Mars, Jupiter, and Saturn — can readily be identified by the backyard astronomer.

As you learn to recognize and follow these five planets, you will discover that they seem to move or "wander" across the sky against a fixed background of more distant stars, varying in position from one month or one season to the next because of their individual orbital motions. Because their orbits around the Sun lie in much the same plane as Earth's orbit, however, the movements of these "wanderers" appear to be confined to a comparatively narrow band across the sky, an area known since ancient times as the *zodiac*. Long before telescopes were invented, ancient astronomers kept careful records of the movements of these five nearest planets in the zodiacal band in relation to the fixed constellations of distant stars, and they came to believe that the motion of the planets had a powerful influence upon human affairs — the original basis for the ancient study of astrology.

The moon, Earth's only natural satellite, also has a regular, cyclic pattern of motion in the sky. The moon orbits the Earth just as the Earth orbits the Sun. Like any of the planets, it has no light of its own but merely reflects the Sun's light to Earth like a huge dull mirror. The amount of the moon's surface that we see at any time, however, depends upon its position in relation to the Earth and the Sun. As it makes a complete circuit of the Earth approximately every twenty-seven days, the moon spends part of the time between the Earth and the Sun, and part of the time on the far side of the Earth from the Sun.

When the moon is on the opposite side of the Earth from the Sun, we see its entire surface illuminated as the full moon; when it lies between the Earth and the Sun, none of the side facing the Earth is illuminated and we see a new moon. At other times, when only part of the side facing the Earth is illuminated, we see the moon in its first quarter, as a half-moon or in its gibbous (convex, or "humped") phase. Whatever the phase we see, however, the same side of the moon is always facing the Earth, for the moon rotates on its axis in exactly the same time that it travels in orbit around the Earth. No one had ever seen the far side of the moon until spacecraft were sent out to take photographs of it.

Other planets also have satellites. The four largest satellites of Jupiter can be distinguished with good binoculars or a small telescope, and as you observe Jupiter you will soon discover that these moons are constantly changing position because of their orbital motion around Jupiter. Mercury and Venus have no satellites, and the two satellites of Mars are so very tiny that they can only be distinguished with large and powerful telescopes. Saturn's largest satellite, Titan, can sometimes be distinguished with a good small telescope, as well as the magnificent system of rings that surrounds that planet and sets it apart from any other celestial object in the sky.

The planets not only move or "wander" across the sky as they travel in their orbits, but can also be seen to vary greatly in brightness from month to month or season to season according to how far away they are. Venus and Mercury can be seen only at certain times when they move out to the side of the Sun in relation to the Earth; when they are behind or in front of the Sun in their orbital travels, they are completely obscured from view in the Sun's fiery glare. Mars, Jupiter, and Saturn appear much larger and brighter in the sky when they are relatively close to the Earth in their orbits (a position known as *opposition*) than when they move around to the far side of the Sun in their orbital travels.

Finally, there are other celestial objects which can occasionally be seen moving in the sky against the background of fixed stars. Comets, for example, travel in huge elongated orbits from far out in the solar system and then swing in close around the Sun and back out again. Bits of space debris known as meteoroids become visible when they enter Earth's atmosphere at terrific speeds and heat to incandescence as they whiz across the sky. Even man-made Earth satellites can sometimes be seen tumbling in their orbits around the Earth.

But in contrast to these nearby members of our Sun's family, the stars themselves lie at enormous distances away from our solar system and thus seem to be fixed in the same locations relative to each other at all times. Of course, we know from centuries of astronomical study that all the stars we can see are actually moving in orbits around the center of the great wheel of stars we know as the Milky Way, the *galaxy* of which our Sun is only one minor member. Yet this galaxy is so huge and its other stars are so very distant from us that no change in their relative position, one to another, is apparent to observers on Earth except over periods of thousands of years. Such familiar constellations as the Big Dipper or Orion, for example, appear much the same to us today as they appeared to stargazers in Biblical times, and they will still appear much the same to observers two thousand years in the future.

This is why it is so important for the amateur astronomer to learn the patterns and locations of certain of the major *constellations*, a word that means, literally, "gatherings of stars." Since the stars in these constellations maintain the same position relative to one another year in and year out, they act as reliable, unchanging guideposts in the sky, pointing the way to multitudes of celestial objects you will want to locate and observe. Thus to locate Arcturus, a huge reddish star that lies comparatively near our own Sun, you need only learn a simple rule: "Follow the handle of the Big Dipper and arc to Arcturus," and you will always be able to find this star anytime that it is above the horizon.

But if the constellations remain fixed relative to each other in the sky, like bright patterns of stars glued to a black velvet background, you will soon see that the whole background seems to move in the course of a night and from season to season. Constellations rise above the horizon, arc across the sky, and then set again — all in a single night. And season by season they slowly shift across the sky, one setting in the west as another rises in the east. For observers in the Northern Hemisphere there is only one fixed reference point, the polestar Polaris, which seems to remain in the same unchanging position in the northern sky night after night and season after season, and even the polestar is seen higher above the northern horizon in the winter than in the summer; its altitude is constant. The other stars and constellations turn in a great circular arc around the polestar during the course of the night as if Polaris were the hub of a great wheel. What is more, many constellations that are visible high in the northern sky on winter nights never rise above the horizon in the summertime, while many southern constellations that are brilliant in the summertime can no longer be seen on winter nights.

The reason for this nightly and seasonal movement of the constellations lies not in any motion of the stars themselves but in the motion of the Earth as it rotates on its axis each day and travels its way around the Sun each year. We know that the Earth turns on its *axis* — an imaginary line running through the Earth from the North Pole to the South Pole — one complete rotation every twenty-four hours. Thus in the course of eight hours of darkness the Earth turns around its axis approximately one-third of a rotation, and the constellations can be seen to rotate around the polestar one-third of a complete arc in the same time. This means that on any given night some stars may be visible in the west early after the Sun goes down but later disappear from sight below the horizon, while other stars rise above the horizon only as the night wears on (see Fig. 2).

At the same time, we know that the Earth in its travels around

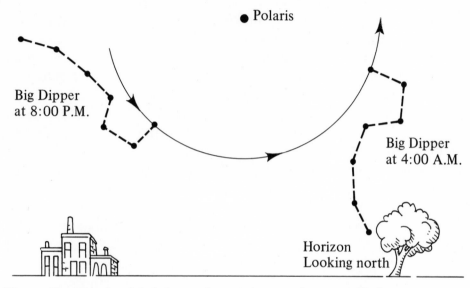

Fig. 2: Nocturnal (nightly) rotation of circumpolar constellations.

the Sun does not stand straight up and down perpendicular to its orbit, but rather is tilted to a perpendicular by approximately 23 degrees. It is this tilt that accounts for the seasonal changes in the constellations that we can see at night as the Earth revolves around the Sun in the course of a year. Certain constellations may be visible from a given observation point only during certain seasons, but not during others when they are above the horizon during daylight hours. Thus to observe some of the constellations, you must learn to pick not only the hours of the night when they will be readily visible, but the season of the year as well.

It might seem that these nightly and seasonal motions of the constellations would be very difficult for the beginning backyard astronomer to learn to follow, but nothing of the sort is true. You can easily learn the pattern a bit at a time, following certain easily recognized key constellations as guides. But the fact that the whole pattern turns in a great nightly and seasonal arc means that there is an ever-changing panorama for you to observe, an incredible and fascinating sky that presents new objects for observation each night, each month, and each season. There is no time, early or late in the evening, spring, summer, fall, or winter that you cannot find some object of fascinating interest to watch and study.

Once you have become familiar with the pattern of stars and constellations, however, you will then need good seasonal star maps to aid you in locating specific objects you may want to observe. Such maps are readily available. For a permanent reference you will want to invest in a good star atlas or astronomical almanac. A number of good ones to choose from, all available at reasonable cost, are listed in the "Additional Reading" section at the end of this book. Many newspapers publish weekly or monthly star maps which can be clipped out and used for handy reference. Such national magazines as *Natural History* (the journal of the American Museum of Natural History) and *Sky and Telescope* publish excellent monthly sky maps, accompanied by notations of the outstanding celestial events that will occur during the month, including the changing positions of the planets, the dates of eclipses of the Sun and moon, the approach of important comets, and the appearance of meteor showers. *The World Almanac* each year also publishes a useful list of forthcoming celestial events.

Most good-sized libraries carry these and many other astronomical references; once you have achieved a basic orientation to the sky, a bit of time spent in your nearest library will provide you with a wealth of information about what can be observed when and under what conditions. And once you have learned which of these references you find most useful, you may want to purchase some of them so that you can have your observational data immediately at your fingertips — an investment that will repay you in many hours of pleasurable viewing.

First, however, a basic orientation to the nighttime sky is essential, and a few simple guidelines will be helpful.

2

MAPPING
THE
HEAVENS

When you first look at an unfamiliar road map, it often appears chaotic and confusing. You know that some order exists, but you cannot see it in the midst of a mass of detail; only when you orient yourself do the details fall into place. So first you must search for orientation points: a familiar city, a state boundary, or a well-known highway. Once you have located a few such points on the map, your initial confusion disappears and the map begins to make some sense.

The same is true of the evening sky. At first it seems filled with a baffling confusion of stars, yet orientation is simple if you can find a few familiar guideposts and then use them step by step to find your way around. Ideally, those guideposts should be objects that remain in the same general area of the sky regardless of the hour or the season. Thus the moon or the planets are of no help because they are constantly moving around against the background of the stars.

No doubt it was a need for fixed and reliable guideposts in the sky that led ancient stargazers to identify and name certain special gatherings of stars which we know today as the *constellations*. Many beginning backyard stargazers shy away from learning the constellations, as if this were a vast and burdensome task — but it is not so difficult as you might think. In all the heavens there are only eighty-eight constellations, including virtually every star that can be seen with the unaided eye. But only forty-eight constellations are visible to observers in the Northern Hemisphere; the remaining forty can be seen only from points below the equator and never become visible in such countries as America or England. And of the forty-eight northern constellations, many are small or unimpressive gatherings of stars that need not command attention. Indeed, as guideposts in the sky, only a very few constellations, perhaps a dozen in all, are really important to know, yet familiarity with those few will enable you to locate almost any other celestial object you might want to find at any season of the year.

● *What Are the Constellations?*
As we look at the sky, it is easy to imagine that such familiar star patterns as the Big Dipper are actually clusters or groups of stars which bear a close relationship to one another. Except in a few instances, however, this is not the case. Stars are far-flung throughout space, with billions, trillions, and quadrillions of miles separating them. Some of the stars in a given constellation may be relatively close to our Sun and its solar system, while others apparently close by in the same constellation may actually be incredibly distant. We cannot, however, directly determine the distances of the stars in a constellation; they all appear like bright pinpoint holes punched in a particular pattern in a sheet of black construction paper held up to the light.

Far-flung as they may be, these stars do have one thing in common. They are all members of our own *galaxy*, a great "island universe" of stars isolated from other galaxies by unimaginable voids of space, and all are moving in enormous orbits around the hub or center of that galaxy just as our own Sun is. Because our galaxy is so huge, however, and because even the nearest other star is so far away from the Sun, we observe no motion of the stars from year to year or even from century to century. The location of any given star in a constellation appears to us to remain the same with respect to the other stars at all times. This is also true for the position of one constellation in relation to the next: once you have learned to identify one, you can always use it as a reference to find others. Thus if you can locate the Big Dipper, you can then always find the polestar Polaris, or the Little Dipper or Cassiopeia or Draco, because these constellations are always located in the same places in relation to the Big Dipper, just as cities on a road map are always located in the same places in relation to each other no matter which way you may turn the map around.

● *Constellations and the Seasons*

All of the northern constellations are not, however, always visible in the sky during all hours of the night or all seasons of the year. Because of the Earth's tilt on its axis as it travels around the Sun, and its rotation on its axis in the course of each day, all the constellations appear to rotate in a great arc in the sky during the course of each night, and many appear to move in a stately parade across the sky from one season to the next. Thus one of the most familiar and interesting of the constellations, Orion the Hunter, is best seen in northern latitudes during the winter months when it is high in the sky early in the evening. During the early summer months, Orion is high in the sky only during daylight hours and has dropped below the horizon by nighttime. The same is true of many other constellations, and one of the excitements of backyard astronomy is to watch the new panorama of stars that becomes visible in the sky with each passing season.

Certain of the constellations, however, are always visible in the northern sky at any season of the year. These are the so-called North Polar Constellations, including some of the most familiar and easily identified of all. These constellations move in a great counterclockwise circle in the sky as the seasons roll by, so that they sometimes appear "upside down" or lying on their sides, but they are always there on any clear dark night. These, then, are the first important guideposts we will use in orienting ourselves to the nighttime sky.

● *The Polar Constellations*

If you were standing directly on the North Pole at night and looked up, you would see a medium-bright star, somewhat isolated

(17)

from the others, directly overhead. This star, known as the North Star, the polestar, or Polaris, is so called because it appears to be directly in line with the polar axis of the Earth, an imaginary line running through the Earth from the South Pole to the North Pole and extending onward into space. Polaris is always visible in the northern sky from anyplace in the Northern Hemisphere; the farther south you may be, the lower it appears in the sky, so that observers on the equator see it on the northern horizon, but it is always in the north. This rather unimpressive star, which might be hard to find except for the help of a nearby constellation, is the stationary hub of a great wheel of North Polar Constellations that can be seen by observers in the United States or England at any season in the year. What is more, when observed from temperate latitudes, these so-called *circumpolar* constellations never drop completely below the horizon so that they can be seen, at least in part, at any hour of the night.

The most familiar of these is Ursa Major, the Great Bear — or at least the rear half of the bear, which we recognize as the Big

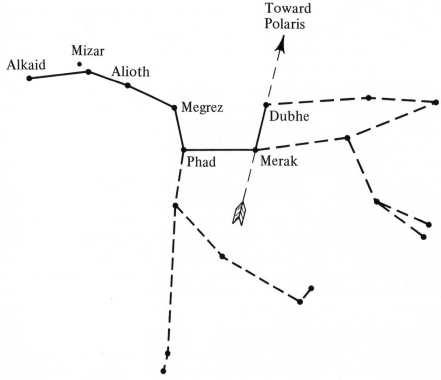

Fig. 3: The Big Dipper.

Dipper (see Fig. 3). This constellation was so familiar and striking, even in ancient times, that the seven stars of the Dipper all have individual names derived from the Arabic, and they are all so important as guideposts to the heavens that we will want to name them. The two bright stars forming the outer edge of the Dipper's bowl are Dubhe and Merak. The star at the bottom of the inner side of the bowl, also bright, is named Phad; a much dimmer star where the handle joins the bowl is Megrez. Moving out on the handle of the dipper are three bright stars, Alioth, Mizar, and Alkaid. Of these, Mizar is a "visual double," which simply means that keen eyes can distinguish a second very faint star lying close to the brighter one.

Why is the Big Dipper so important to stargazers? Because to all who recognize it, it is a remarkable key to the polar heavens. Merak and Dubhe are particularly familiar as the "pointers," for an imaginary arrow drawn through these two stars and followed out will point almost directly to Polaris, as seen in Figure 4. Although the North Star appears rather small and lonely as the hub of the northern heavens, a close look will reveal that it forms the end of the handle of a smaller dipper, the constellation of Ursa Minor, more familiar as the Little Dipper. All the stars of this constellation excepting Polaris and Kochab (the star at the rim of the Dipper) are comparatively faint and unimpressive, so it is never as easy to see as the Big Dipper. But you can always find it if you remember that it is upside down to the Big Dipper, as if the small Dipper were being emptied into the big one.

Merak and Dubhe are not the only useful "pointers" to be found in the Big Dipper. In Figure 5 we see that a number of other stars and constellations can be found with the aid of other Dipper stars as "pointers." (In using this and the other "guidepost" drawings in this book, remember that the constellations shown are drawn to a very small scale in order to show a wide segment of the sky. They will appear much, much larger when you see them in the nighttime sky. The Big Dipper, for example, stretches out over a quarter of the sky, and the stars of other constellations may seem surprisingly widely spaced.) First, draw an imaginary line from Alioth, the closest "handle" star to the bowl of the Dipper, to Polaris and on equally far beyond. This line will then reach to a group of stars, all moderately bright, shaped like an inverted letter *W* in the sky. This is the constellation Cassiopeia, sometimes

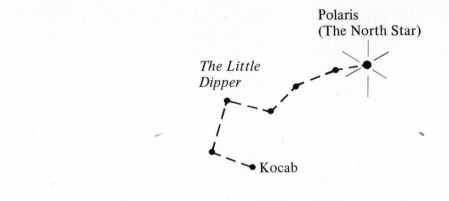

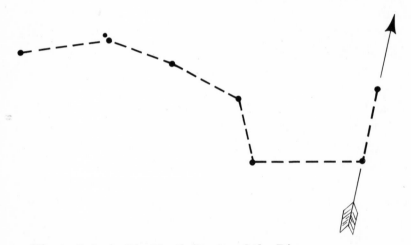

Fig. 4: Polaris (the North Star) and the Dippers.

known as Cassiopeia's Chair — one of the many constellations named for gods and other personalities from Greek mythology. Next, draw an imaginary line across the top of the Big Dipper from Megrez through Dubhe and extend it. Eventually you will come to Capella, one of the brightest of all the stars in the sky. Capella is a striking yellow star which appears, during winter months, to be located in the zenith — directly overhead at night. Some distance below Capella when the Big Dipper is upright you will find the twin stars Castor and Pollux, the major bright stars in the constellation Gemini, the Twins.

Two other circumpolar constellations and three important
bright stars that are landmarks in the sky can also be identified
with the help of Figure 5, using the Big Dipper and the Little
Dipper as guideposts. One is Draco, the Dragon, a long, sprawling

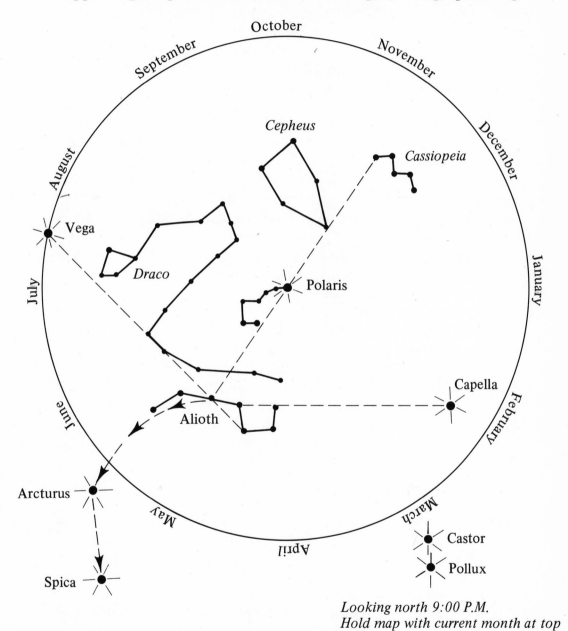

Looking north 9:00 P.M.
Hold map with current month at top

Fig. 5: The circumpolar constellations.

constellation with an irregular triangle forming the head and a tail swinging in a long curve around the polar wheel to end immediately between the Big Dipper and the Little Dipper. You can find Draco best by locating these "tail stars," the only comparatively bright stars between the two Dippers, and following them around in the direction of the Big Dipper's handle and on into an arc around the Little Dipper. Between Draco's head and Cassiopeia is the constellation Cepheus, shaped like a rectangle wearing a dunce cap — a somewhat more difficult constellation to identify than the others. Among the major stars, the bright star named Vega, a brilliant blue-white star which appears directly overhead on summer nights, is visible out beyond Draco's head from the polestar.

If you follow the curve of the Big Dipper's handle and continue the same arc on beyond Alkaid, you will presently reach the extremely bright and distinctly reddish-colored star, Arcturus, in the constellation of Boötes, the Herdsman, and if the arc is followed on beyond Arcturus about the same distance, it will reach the almost equally bright Spica. Bear in mind that all of these denizens of the polar sky are not always visible all of the time; the farther from the polestar you look in any direction, the greater the likelihood that the constellations, or portions of them, will be below the horizon part of the time. But with a little careful observation on a few successive evenings, perhaps at different hours, you will soon become familiar with these polar constellations, and will make an important discovery: that with certain familiar landmarks to guide you, the confusion of stars begins to fall into recognizable patterns, and that the more time you spend observing the sky, the more detail becomes clear.

● *The Stars of Springtime*
Certain important guidepost constellations appear in the sky in the late winter and early spring. One of the most impressive of these, and a useful guide to finding others, is Leo, the Lion, which lies to the east of the Big Dipper (see Fig. 6). Leo is a huge constellation made up of two main groups of stars: a sickle-shaped group marking his head and shoulders, and a triangular group forming his hindquarters. Again, stars of the Big Dipper provide a handy guide for locating Leo. By drawing a line through Megrez

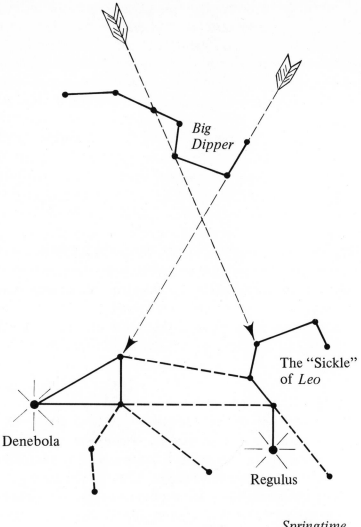

Big Dipper

The "Sickle" of *Leo*

Denebola

Regulus

Springtime Looking south

Fig. 6: Locating Leo in springtime.

and Phad, the stars that form the back of the Dipper's bowl, and following that line southeasterly (away from the Little Dipper), you will come to the so-called "sickle of Leo," the Lion's head. Another imaginary line drawn through Dubhe and Merak, the Polaris "pointers," but extended in the opposite direction, will bring you to the triangle that forms the back part of Leo, as in Figure 6.

(23)

Identification of these two parts of the constellation is further simplified by the presence of an impressive star located in each part. In the handle of the "sickle" is an extremely bright star known as Regulus; in the triangle there is a slightly less bright star, Denebola. With a little imagination you can piece these parts of this constellation together and picture a giant lion striding across the sky.

With Leo identified as a center, four other spring constellations can be found encircling him in clockwise fashion (see Fig. 7). Above him and forming a triangle with the Big Dipper is the constellation Gemini with the bright "twin stars," Castor and Pollux. These two striking stars lie quite close together, a rather unusual situation in the sky. South of Leo is a long, sprawling, serpent-like curve of stars twice as long as Draco which forms the constellation Hydra, the Serpent. On the opposite side of Leo from Gemini you can again locate the bright stars, Arcturus and Spica. Arcturus is the brightest star in the constellation of Boötes, the Herdsman, and Spica is your guide to Virgo, the Virgin — a group of stars which form a huge capital *Y* with Spica at the bottom of the stem.

● *The Summer Constellations*
These star groups are somewhat more difficult to identify and will test your growing skill in finding your way about the heavens. A good place to start is with Boötes and its orange-red star Arcturus as a guidepost (see Fig. 8). A little to the east of Boötes you will see a brilliant half-circle of seven stars which lie close together and appear to form a semicircular crown. This small, gemlike constellation is the Corona Borealis or Northern Crown, unmistakable and brilliant. Continuing east you will find a much more dim and sprawling constellation, Hercules, best identified by the uneven square of four stars forming its center.

Still farther east from Hercules is a huge triangle of three very bright stars. As summer progresses, these three stars are seen almost directly overhead, and each one is a key to a different constellation. Closest to Hercules and near the head of Draco is brilliant Vega in the constellation of Lyra, the Lyre. North and east of Lyra is Cygnus, the Swan, marked by the brilliant star Deneb;

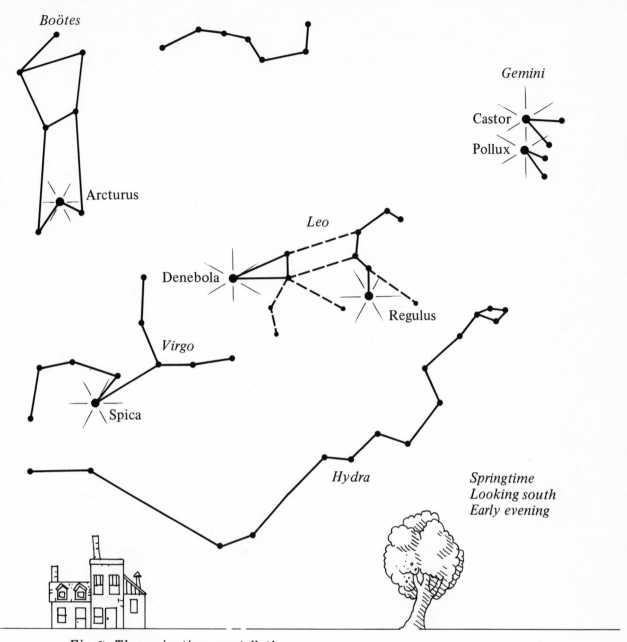

Fig. 7: The springtime constellations.

and south and east is Aquila, the Eagle, containing another striking star named Altair. In the southern sky below Hercules is the
roughly oval-shaped constellation Ophiuchus, and still farther

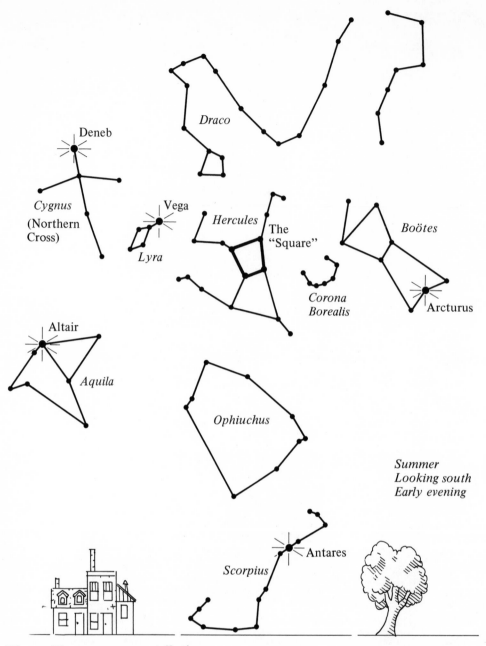

Fig. 8: The summer constellations.

south, just above the horizon in the summer, is the brilliant constellation Scorpius, shaped rather like a fishhook in the sky. Scorpius is notable for a bright and distinctly red star known as Antares.

● *The Sky in Autumn*

By early autumn the two Dippers and the other North Polar Constellations will have rotated a full 180 degrees around Polaris
from their positions in early spring, and the springtime constella-

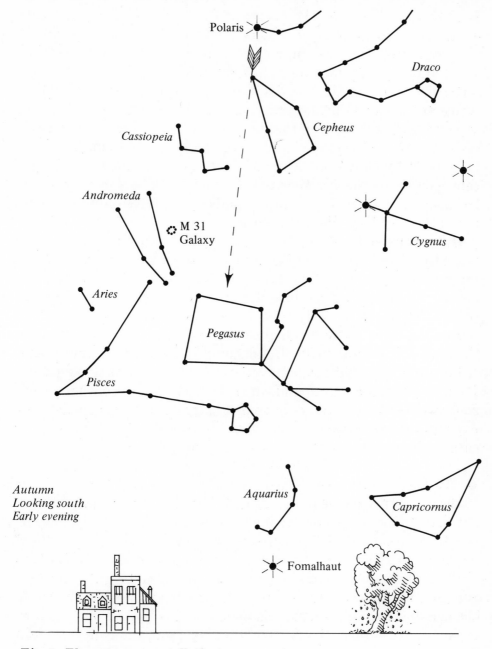

Autumn
Looking south
Early evening

Fig. 9: The autumn constellations.

tions will have vanished below the horizon. The new autumn constellations are somewhat dim and difficult to identify (see Fig. 9). If you draw a line south from Polaris and extend it between Cassiopeia and Cepheus, you will come to a huge uneven square which forms the main body of the constellation Pegasus, the Winged Horse. Between Pegasus and Cassiopeia are two long lines of stars that form the constellation Andromeda. If you look closely at this constellation, you may be able to see an odd, fuzzy patch of light, almost like a star but not as sharply defined. As we will see later, this patch of light is not a star at all but actually another whole and separate island universe, the Andromeda Galaxy, that lies far, far beyond any of the stars in our own Milky Way. This is one of the three so-called "naked-eye" galaxies that can be distinguished without the aid of magnifying lenses, and the only one thus visible in the Northern Hemisphere. (The other two, the Greater and Lesser Magellanic Clouds, are visible only to observers in the Southern Hemisphere.)

Other constellations in the autumn sky — Capricornus, Aquarius, Pisces, and Aries, among others — seem rather dull and unimpressive because they contain relatively few bright stars. They are chiefly of interest because they are among the so-called *zodiacal constellations*, to be discussed later.

As for bright stars in the autumn sky, there is really only one that calls attention to itself, although the brilliant trio Vega, Altair, and Deneb are still visible to the west. A line drawn from Polaris through Pegasus and carried almost to the southern horizon will lead you to the only really bright star characteristic of autumn, a star named Fomalhaut, often difficult to identify because it lies so close to the southern horizon.

● *The Constellations of Winter*
If the autumn skies seem rather dull, the situation is quite different in the winter, for now we find a splendid and exciting array of constellations (see Fig. 10). By far the most prominent of them all, high in the sky early in the evening, is mighty Orion, the Hunter. Orion is easy to identify from the three bright stars in a row that form the hunter's belt. Two widely extended stars above the belt and two below mark his arms and his legs, and a close-set string of stars form the dagger hanging from his belt. You will

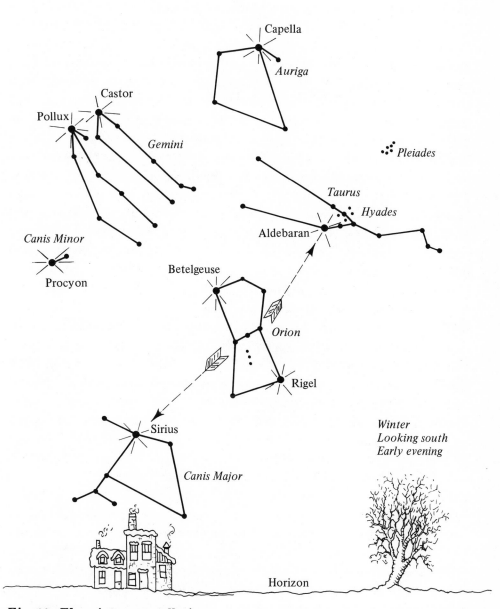

Polaris

Casseiopea

Capella

Auriga

Castor

Pollux

Gemini

Pleiades

Taurus

Hyades

Aldebaran

Canis Minor

Procyon

Betelgeuse

Orion

Rigel

Sirius

Canis Major

Winter
Looking south
Early evening

Horizon

Fig. 10: The winter constellations.

(29)

immediately notice that two of the stars in Orion, one marking a shoulder and the other the opposite foot, are among the brightest stars to be found anywhere in the sky. The shoulder star can be seen to be distinctly red-orange in color, a supergiant named Betelgeuse. This is a so-called "variable star" because it appears to be considerably brighter at some times than at others. Diagonally from Betelgeuse and below the hunter's belt is Rigel, a brilliant blue-white star that gleams like a perfect diamond.

These are by no means the only bright stars in the winter sky, however, and the stars of Orion will serve as handy guides to help you find and identify several others. If you draw a line through the stars in Orion's belt and extend it to the southeast, you will come to a singularly brilliant star. This is Sirius, the Dog Star, so called because it is the major star in the constellation Canus Major, the Big Dog. Astronomers recognize Sirius as the brightest star anywhere in the heavens. If you draw a line from this star through the middle belt star of Orion and extend it an equal distance farther, you will reach a V-shaped group of stars in the constellation Taurus, the Bull, dominated by a very bright red star named Aldebaran. Extend the same line still farther and you will come to a small cluster of stars, some seven of which seem to be grouped very closely together — the Pleiades. Going back to Orion and following a line drawn eastward from Betelgeuse, you will find the constellation Canus Minor, the Little Dog, made up of only two stars but including one bright one, the striking Procyon. Betelgeuse, Sirius, and Procyon form an impressive brilliant triangle of stars in the sky.

Nor are these all. By drawing a line from Rigel through Betelgeuse and extending it farther, we come to our old friends Castor and Pollux, while a line drawn from Rigel northward between Betelgeuse in Orion and Aldebaran in Taurus will ultimately lead to bright yellow Capella in the five-sided constellation Auriga, the Charioteer.

The constellations we have discussed above are only a few of the many that exist, landmark constellations that seem to dominate the sky as season follows season. As you become familiar with them, other less striking constellations will also fall in place. But with just these "guidepost" constellations alone, you will be able to locate a multitude of fascinating objects in the sky, whether you are observing with unaided vision, with binoculars, or with a telescope. Before ending our orientation tour, however, we should mention two other aspects of the sky at least briefly: the rather special star groupings known as the Constellations of the Zodiac; and the strange and spectacular "river of stars" that can be seen crossing some portion of the sky at any season of the year, the phenomenon that puts everything else that we see in the sky into its proper perspective — the Milky Way.

● *The Zodiacal Constellations*

What is the zodiac? The word arises from Greek and Latin terms meaning "circle of living things," and the zodiac is an area in which science, pseudo-science, history, and mythology become inextricably entangled. The term refers to a special narrow belt across the sky and encircling the earth which ancient stargazers considered singularly important. This beltlike area lies in the plane of the ecliptic — the plane of the Earth's orbit around the Sun. During the daytime it is the path that the Sun seems to follow across the sky; at night it is the path in which the moon rises, travels, and sets. It was here, too, within this narrow belt that the ancient astronomers always found the five "wandering planets" — Mercury, Venus, Mars, Jupiter, and Saturn.

The zodiac is also the portion of the sky in which twelve particular constellations can be seen, the so-called zodiacal constellations. Each month one of these twelve appears above the horizon in the east, rising a little higher in the sky night after night, month after month until it has completely crossed the sky and disappeared below the horizon in the west. Meanwhile, each month, a new zodiacal constellation appears in the east, to form a year-long procession marching across the sky. Ancient peoples believed that these particular constellations and the planets which appeared to move about among them had great influence upon the lives of men and the events of history. They developed complicated formulas involving the position of the zodiacal constellations in relation to the planets at various times during the year as a means of trying to foretell the future — the birth of *astrology*, a term which means simply "study of the stars."

Today astronomers regard astrology as a pseudo-science in the same class as alchemy, the ancient and misguided search for a way to turn base metals into gold by chemical means. But to the backyard astronomer certain of the zodiacal constellations are important guideposts in the sky and are a great help in locating the planets throughout the year. Among these, the constellations of Leo, Gemini, Scorpius, and Taurus, already discussed, are quite striking and easy to identify. Others such as Aries (the Ram), Aquarius (the Water Carrier), or Sagittarius (the Archer) are more difficult to distinguish, but you will be able to identify them when you become more familiar with the night sky.

When you use detailed star maps for finding special objects in the sky, you will often find that reference is made to these zodiacal constellations. For example, when the seasonal star map indicates that "Jupiter is visible in Virgo in mid-July," this simply means that the planet Jupiter will be seen as an especially bright "extra star" in the constellation of Virgo at the month and time designated.

● *The Galactic River*
No discussion of guideposts in the sky would be complete without mention of the hazy band of gentle white light that arches across the sky, visible during any season of the year. Ancient Greek stargazers thought it looked like a river of milk; today we call this band of light the Milky Way and recognize it as what we can see of an enormous cluster of stars making up the *galaxy* (from the Greek word meaning milk) of which our Sun is a part.

The Milky Way is actually nothing more nor less than a great band of uncountable millions of stars in the sky, most of them so faint that they cannot be separated or distinguished by the naked eye at all. Rather, they appear as a ghostly band of hazy light visible on any clear dark night of the year but are most striking of all during the late summer. To see it well, you must pick a moonless night and observe from someplace far from house lights, streetlights, or city sky glow. If you dark-adapt your eyes, the Milky Way will stand out even more remarkably, and you will be able to distinguish patches of lightness and darkness within the stream. Even so, however, you will not really appreciate the striking beauty of the Milky Way until you look at it through binoculars and discover for yourself the countless swarms of very faint stars that make up this hazy band of light.

No one knows how many stars there are in the Milky Way; astronomers estimate as many as one hundred billion or more. In addition, there are great clouds of dust and gas swirling between the stars, known to astronomers as *nebulae*. Some of these gas and dust clouds are themselves luminous, while others are dark and obscure many of the stars from view. But all of these stars and the intervening gas and dust clouds are part of a single galaxy, a huge spiral-shaped "island universe" made up of stars and other thinly dispersed solid matter. Our own Sun lies near the outer edge of this galaxy on one of its spiral arms; virtually all the other stars that we can see in the sky are also part of this galaxy and are clearly distinguishable to us as individual stars only because they lie closer to us than the stars in other portions of the galaxy.

What we see as the Milky Way is, in fact, a sort of edge-on view of this vast island universe, observed from a point near one edge and looking toward the thickly star-populated center. If we could move completely away from the galaxy and observe it from an enormous distance, we would see that it is shaped like a huge disk, thin at the edges and thicker at the middle, with many spiraling arms of gas and stars trailing out from a dense glowing hub.

Just as the Earth travels in an orbit around the Sun, the Sun travels in an orbit around the center of the galaxy. What is more, the whole galaxy is itself slowly rotating around its axis. Astronomers know that the Sun is traveling at a speed of approximately 140 miles per second in its orbit around the center of the galaxy, yet this island universe of stars is so huge and the Sun is so far from the center that it takes two hundred million years to make a single circuit.

The Milky Way is not, of course, the only galaxy in the universe. There are millions, perhaps billions of others scattered throughout space on all sides of us. Most of these, however, are far too distant and faint for the amateur astronomer to distinguish with the unaided eye or with low-powered lenses. Only the great galaxy in Andromeda and the Greater and Lesser Magellanic Clouds can be distinguished with ease, and it was only a few decades ago that astronomers realized that these objects really were entire galaxies of stars much the same as our Milky Way. For many years these hazy objects in the sky were believed merely to be luminous clouds of gas within our own galaxy, and for practical purposes all of the heavenly bodies you will be observing as a backyard astronomer will indeed be objects that are part of our own Milky Way galaxy. Yet the sight of the Milky Way itself, stretched in glowing splendor across the sky, at least gives us a hint of the incredible magnitude of the universe that stretches out beyond our own galaxy into the vast reaches of space, as far as our greatest telescopes can probe and even farther.

A basic orientation to the sky is extremely important as you begin your exploration of the nighttime heavens. With a little time, practice, and patience you will soon be able to familiarize yourself with the guideposts that we have discussed, so that any month of the year you can find your way about. And just as the constellations themselves can be identified and studied with the unaided eye, so many other fascinating celestial objects and displays can be observed without any special instruments or equipment. In the next chapter we shall consider some of these objects in more detail, particularly those in our own immediate neighborhood in space: the Sun and the planets that make up our solar system.

3

UNAIDED-EYE
OBSERVATION

When we speak of astronomical observation many people immediately think of telescopes. Yet some of the most exciting displays to be seen in the heavens can actually be observed best with the unaided eye. In identifying the constellations and major "landmark stars," a telescope or even binoculars would be more hindrance than help. Among other celestial phenomena that can be best observed with unaided vision are eclipses and occultations, the movement of the planets in the sky, the appearance of comets, the meteor showers that periodically create celestial fireworks displays, and the observation of man-made Earth satellites.

● *Eclipses of the Moon*
If you were watching the sky on the evening of January 30, 1972, you may have witnessed one of the most fascinating and dramatic celestial events of that year. It was a chilly winter night, clear and bright in many parts of the United States, with a full moon gleaming high in the sky. Then, shortly after midnight, a remarkable change took place. A dark, semicircular notch appeared in the

edge of the moon's bright face, quite without warning, exactly as if someone had begun to nibble away at the disk. Slowly this dark semicircle enlarged and advanced across the face of the moon as if the tip of a thumb were pushing its way across the silvery disk. As more and more of the moon was engulfed by the creeping shadow, the night became perceptibly darker until the last trace of moonlight disappeared from the sky. All that could be seen was a dull, coppery shadow in the sky where the moon had been, barely distinguishable from the darkness around it. And then, as gradually as the shadow advanced across the moon, it passed on and began to recede. First a brilliant crescent edge of moonlight appeared; then, slowly, the shadow moved away until the whole face of the full moon was shining again, approximately two hours after the shadow first appeared.

A total eclipse of the moon is an awesome sight to observe. Even the modern stargazer who understands what is happening will find it curiously disturbing to watch. Thus we can understand the fear and confusion of primitive people who watched the eclipsing moon with no idea why it came about. No wonder they regarded this apparently inexplicable darkening of the moon as an omen of ill fortune and evil changes in the affairs of men! Even when astronomers later came to recognize what actually was happening — that the moon was merely passing through a cone of shadow cast into space when the Earth passed between it and the Sun — lunar eclipses were still regarded with uneasiness, and the superstitious believed that these were the times when demons were released and spirits roamed the earth.

A glance at Figure 11A will show clearly what happens when a lunar eclipse occurs. The moon is a satellite body orbiting the Earth approximately once every twenty-seven days. We know now that the plane of the moon's orbit around the Earth is very close to the plane of the ecliptic — that is, the plane of the Earth's orbit around the Sun. Thus during part of its twenty-seven-day journey around the Earth, the moon passes between the Earth and the Sun, while somewhat later it passes on the far side of the Earth from the Sun.

We see this regular movement of the moon around the Earth reflected in the changing phases of the moon from one day to the next throughout the month. When the moon is directly between the Earth and the Sun — the new moon phase — we see no bright image at all, since the moon generates no light of its own but shines only by reflected sunlight. Then as it moves slightly out of alignment between the Earth and the Sun, we see the waxing crescent phase appear. Day by day more and more of the lighted moon surface becomes visible as it moves farther around the Earth until it finally reaches the far side of the Earth from the Sun. At that point the whole surface is illuminated, the phase we know as the full moon.

We can also see that if the moon passes into perfect alignment with the Earth and the Sun at the time of the full moon, it would have to pass through a cone of shadow thrown out into space by the Earth. When such an event occurs during our daylight hours, we see nothing, since the moon is on the far side of the Earth from us at the crucial moment. But when it occurs at night, we see the

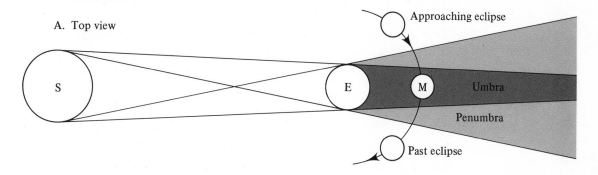

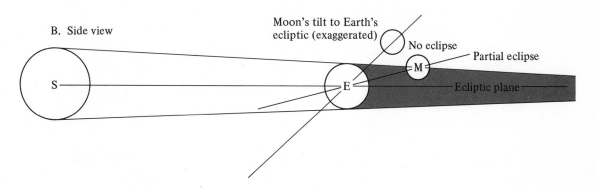

Fig. 11: Eclipses of the moon (not to scale).

(37)

Earth's shadow pass across the face of the moon as a lunar eclipse.

Why, then, is an eclipse of the moon not visible from someplace on Earth at each full moon? If the plane of the moon's orbit around the Earth were *exactly* the same as the plane of Earth's orbit around the Sun, there would indeed be an eclipse every month. In fact, however, the moon's orbit is tilted at a slight angle from the Earth's ecliptic plane (see Fig. 11B) so it is only when the moon happens to cross Earth's ecliptic at full-moon phase that an eclipse will occur; at other times, the moon will miss the Earth's shadow altogether. As it is, the conditions for a lunar eclipse actually occur with surprising frequency. On the average, an eclipse of the moon will be visible either completely or partly in the United States once or twice each year — completely visible when the eclipsing moon is high in the sky at night, partly visible if it is low on the horizon so that it rises or sets while the eclipse is in progress. Thus you will have frequent opportunities to observe lunar eclipses over the years. Usually forthcoming eclipses are announced well ahead of time in the newspapers. As mentioned earlier, you can also find the dates of forthcoming lunar eclipses listed in *The World Almanac* under "Eclipses" or "Celestial Events," as well as in such sources as *Natural History* magazine or *Sky and Telescope.*

Referring back to Figures 11A and 11B, it is easy to see that an eclipse of the moon can occur only at full moon, and will be visible from anywhere on one complete hemisphere of the Earth when it occurs, providing the sky is clear. But all eclipses of the moon are not total eclipses. Because the Sun is a huge light source, Earth's shadow has two distinct portions: a comparatively narrow cone of dark shadow known as the *umbra* and a much wider cone of partial shadow called the *penumbra.* If the moon passes into the center of the umbra during an eclipse, the eclipse is total. If it is slightly above or below the umbra so that only a part of the moon passes through this cone of dark shadow, the eclipse will be partial. At other times, when the moon passes still farther above or below the umbra, it may miss the dark shadow altogether and merely pass through the faint half-shadow of the penumbra. So-called "penumbral eclipses" are easy to miss because the dimming of the moon's light is not too impressive and there is no sharp crescent shadow moving across the moon's face. However, the attentive observer can detect a penumbral eclipse as a less spectacular but still interesting phenomenon.

Oddly enough, the moon rarely becomes completely invisible even in the midst of a total umbral eclipse in which the whole surface lies completely in the cone of dark shadow for over an hour. At such times, the disk of the moon can usually still be seen as a dim, copper-colored circle in the sky. This is so because the Sun's rays are bent or refracted by the Earth's thick layer of atmospheric gases and a small amount of this light from the Sun still reaches the moon's surface even during a total eclipse. How well this dim "shadow moon" can be seen during any given eclipse, however, depends upon atmospheric conditions on Earth. There have been eclipses in which the moon has disappeared so completely that it could not be seen at all, while at other times the totally eclipsed moon was still so bright that it was difficult to believe that an eclipse was occurring. Volcanic gas, dust or smoke from forest fires, for example, can block the passage of refracted sunlight through Earth's atmosphere and make one eclipse notably darker than another.

Today we know that eclipses of the moon have no significant effects here on Earth, but they may indeed have earthshaking effects on the moon itself. Since the moon has no atmosphere of its own, the passing of the sunlit side into the Earth's shadow causes a sudden and dramatic drop in the surface temperature of the moon, as much as 100 degrees Fahrenheit or more in the course of a single hour. Since solid material on the moon's surface tends to expand when warmed and to contract when chilled, just as anywhere else, the sudden drop in temperature during a lunar eclipse followed by the sudden rise in temperature when the eclipse is over may well cause microscopic cracks to form in the crystalline structure of the rock of the moon's mountains.

Astronomers today believe that abrupt temperature changes during lunar eclipses have been responsible for a great deal of the erosion of lunar mountains and craters. Some have even suggested that the abrupt cooling and rewarming may produce observable effects on the surface of the moon. Thus many amateur astronomers who are thoroughly acquainted with the moon's surface features study the moon very carefully with telescopes during and immediately after total eclipses.

● *Solar Eclipses*

Spectacular as they are, lunar eclipses seem like minor curiosities compared to eclipses of the Sun. Solar eclipses occur when the moon itself moves into a straight line between the Earth and the Sun and casts its shadow on a small portion of the Earth's surface. Of course the Sun is immensely larger than the moon, but the moon in its orbit around the Earth is so much closer than the Sun that the two heavenly bodies appear almost exactly the same size in the sky. Thus when the three bodies are perfectly aligned, with the moon in the middle, a circle of shadow ranging from 50 to 150 miles in diameter appears on the surface of the Earth. Because the Earth is rotating on its axis, this patch of shadow moves swiftly across the Earth's surface, much as the shadow of an airplane moves across a field on a sunny day, marking a path of shadow several thousand miles long from the beginning of the eclipse to the end.

This shadowy path, known as the "path of total eclipse" or "path of totality," is the only area on the Earth's surface from which a total eclipse of the Sun can be observed, and of course it varies widely from one eclipse to the next (see Fig. 12). From any single point along the path of totality during an eclipse, the surface of the Sun will be seen to be obscured for a period ranging from two to seven minutes as the moon appears to pass across the face of the Sun.

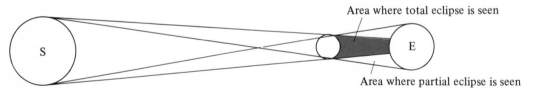

Fig. 12: Eclipses of the Sun (not to scale).

Astronomers will often travel great distances in order to be in a favorable position to observe a total eclipse, but even then observation may be difficult depending on the path of totality. The solar eclipse that occurred on July 10, 1972, was one of the most difficult in history to observe, since its path of totality extended from Siberia across northern Alaska, northern Canada, and out across the Atlantic over Nova Scotia — all areas where there are relatively few people and even fewer good stations for observation. The next eclipse, which occurred on June 30, 1973, was not visible from any point in North America, since the path of totality traced a line across North Africa. Fortunately for the backyard astronomer, however, there is an area some two thousand miles wide on either side of the path of totality in which a partial eclipse of the Sun can be observed, and even this is a remarkable sight to see.

Those fortunate enough to observe a total solar eclipse are treated to an eerie spectacle indeed. In the middle of a bright, sunny day the sunlight suddenly begins to fade away, dimmer and dimmer, not into total darkness but to a strange unnatural twilight. The blue sky darkens to purple, then almost to black, and suddenly the stars can be seen! At the moment that the moon completely hides the Sun's bright disk, the great fiery halo of incandescent gas surrounding the Sun, normally invisible because of the much greater glare of the Sun's disk, suddenly leaps into view — a glorious *corona* of pearly light, sometimes marked with splendid long red streamers or *prominences* of incandescent gas spearing out horizontally from the Sun's surface and then curving downward again like enormous fiery snakes. Then, as the moon moves on, there is a brilliant flare of yellow light as the Sun's disk begins to emerge. Quickly the sky turns blue again, the stars vanish, and within a few minutes full daylight is once again restored.

Even those who can see only a partial eclipse of the Sun can still witness an exciting phenomenon. The moon can be seen to obscure a portion of the Sun's disk like the tip of a giant finger moving across the surface of the Sun. If as much as 30 percent of the disk is obscured, there will be a perceptible dimming of daylight, and a number of curious phenomena can be observed. For example, in any area where the Sun shines through foliage, allowing a mottling of sunlight and shadow to reach the ground, you will see multitudes of tiny images of the partially obscured Sun flickering in the dappled light, and a piece of cardboard with a pinhole cut in it will throw an image of the partly obscured Sun, like a replica of the Sun with a bite taken out of it, on a sheet of white paper held beneath it.

This, in fact, is the only perfectly safe way to observe a partial eclipse of the Sun, for there is very real danger to the eyes if you attempt to observe a partial eclipse by gazing directly at the Sun without taking great care to screen your eyes from the damaging light rays. *Never use any kind of optical instrument during a solar eclipse*; your eyes could be irreparably damaged in a matter of seconds. Even so-called "sun filters" are dangerous for anyone but an expert astronomer to use.

To observe a solar eclipse safely, take a sheet of thin cardboard and, with a hot needle, burn a round "pinhole" about one-eighth inch in diameter in the center. Then during the eclipse, stand with your back to the Sun, hold the sheet of cardboard up beside you as in Figure 13, with a sheet of white paper beneath it. The cardboard will act like the diaphragm of a pinhole camera, allowing a circle of light to pass through. By moving the white paper up or down, you can bring an image of the eclipsing Sun into sharp focus and will be able to follow the progress of the moon's disk

Eclipsing
sun

Cardboard with pinhole

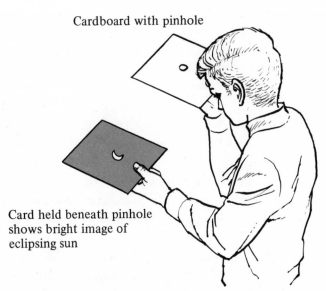

Card held beneath pinhole
shows bright image of
eclipsing sun

Fig. 13: Indirect observation of a solar eclipse.

(42)

across the face of the Sun from beginning to end in perfect safety.

If you insist upon a more direct view of the eclipsing Sun, you must prepare in advance an effective Sun shield for your eyes. Open a large-size roll of black-and-white film in broad daylight, exposing it completely. Then develop the film in your own darkroom, or have it developed commercially, marking the envelope, "Purposely overexposed; develop completely." The film, when developed, should be a dense, uniform black, but you will find that you can still see the image of an electric light bulb through it if you hold it close to the bulb. *Two layers* of this overexposed film will make a reasonably safe screen for your eyes in observing a partial eclipse. Most amateur observers who have witnessed a solar eclipse, however, will testify that indirect observation by means of a pinhole in a cardboard screen, as described above, will provide at least as good a view of the spectacle, if not better, without posing even a remote threat to your eyesight.

Why are professional astronomers so interested in solar eclipses that they will travel halfway around the world to observe them? During the brief period of a total eclipse, there is an opportunity to perform many experiments that simply cannot be done at any other-time. For example, a total eclipse offers astronomers a brief opportunity to study the nature and composition of the Sun's outer atmosphere or *corona*. Solar prominences and other surface phenomena can be studied best under these conditions too.

During a total eclipse in the year 1917, physicists were able to demonstrate that light rays from a distant star are bent slightly when they pass very close to a massive heavenly body such as the Sun — a phenomenon that Albert Einstein had earlier predicted in his general theory of relativity. More recently, astronomers have used total solar eclipses as an opportunity to search for evidence of the elusive planet Vulcan, a tiny (and still hypothetical) planetary body believed by some astronomers to travel in orbit around the Sun far closer than even the innermost planet Mercury. An astronomer named William Henry Pickering first thought that he had detected such a tiny innermost planet back in the 1930s, and even named it Vulcan after the Roman god of fire. No one else was ever able to confirm his sighting, but it seemed likely that if such a planet existed, it must be so small, and lie so close to the Sun, that it would be totally obscured by the Sun's glare at all times except during a total eclipse. In 1970 two American astronomers thought that they, too, had found evidence of an intra-Mercurian planet, but again their sighting could not be confirmed by anyone else. Even today we are still not sure that a planet Vulcan actually exists, but if it does, the best time for astronomers to observe it would be during a total eclipse of the Sun.

● *Occultations*

Still another phenomenon that can be observed with the unaided eye, or with a good pair of binoculars, is the occasional occultation or "hiding" of a bright star or one of the planets by the moon in its travels in the sky. An occultation occurs any time that the moon's disk moves in front of a more distant heavenly body, thus obscuring it from view, but occultations of prominent stars or planets occur less commonly than one might imagine.

During the year 1972, for example, Venus was occulted or hidden by the moon only once, and Mercury, Mars, and Jupiter were each occulted only twice in the course of the year, even though these planets all move in the same zodiacal band of the heavens as the moon. Between 1967 and 1972, the ruddy star Antares in the constellation Scorpio lay directly in the moon's path and was occulted by the moon nearly every month and sometimes twice in a month. Because of a slight periodical shift in the plane of the moon's orbit around the Earth, this long series of occultations of Antares came to an end in 1972 and will not resume again until 1986, but in the meantime occultations of other bright stars in the zodiacal constellations will occur from time to time, including Aldebaran, Pollux, Spica, and Regulus. *The World Almanac* each year carries a listing of dates of interesting planetary and star occultations in its "Celestial Events" calendar.

Although occultations of stars and planets can be observed either with the unaided eye or with binoculars, these events are even more interesting to watch with a good small telescope. Because planets such as Venus, Mars, or Jupiter show definite disks in the telescope, it is possible to watch their planetary disks be slowly obscured by the moon as the occultation occurs. In the case of stars, the picture is different. Even the brightest star is never seen as anything but a pinpoint of light in any telescope, so that the occultation of a star appears to occur instantaneously. As the time of an occultation approaches, you can see the moon's disk moving up to the star until suddenly, without the slightest flicker, the star's light blinks out. As the moon moves on, you will presently see the star reappear at the other side just as suddenly as it vanished. This abrupt disappearance and reappearance of a star occulted by the moon, incidentally, provides clear evidence that the moon has no atmosphere. If there were an atmosphere, the star being occulted would be seen to grow dim and flicker as the edge or *limb* of the moon approached it, since the star's light passing through that atmosphere would be obscured gradually. The fact that this does not happen, and that the starlight simply blinks out as the edge of the moon moves across it, indicates that there is no significant envelope of atmospheric gas surrounding the moon at all.

● *The Movement of the Planets*
Of the five planets of our Sun's solar system which can be readily identified with the unaided eye and followed from season to season — Mercury, Venus, Mars, Jupiter, and Saturn — each has features of special interest for the backyard astronomer.

MERCURY. Smallest of the Sun's planets and the closest to the Sun, Mercury never strays from the zodiacal belt, since the plane of its orbit around the Sun is only slightly tilted from the Earth's plane of the ecliptic. But Mercury never strays far from the Sun either, and this means that it can only be seen by looking toward the Sun and can thus be very difficult to identify. When the Sun is above the horizon, the little planet will be lost in its glare, so the search for Mercury must be carried out immediately after sunset or immediately before sunrise at times when the planet is in a favorable position for viewing — that is, when it is far to one side or the other of the Sun, a position that astronomers speak of as *elongation* (see Fig. 14). Because Mercury travels around the Sun very swiftly, making a complete circuit in just eighty-eight days, the periods of greatest elongation, first to the east of the Sun and then to the west, occur approximately forty-four days apart, and at best it will be visible for only a few days at each elongation. Detailed calendars of celestial events will provide the dates that Mercury can most readily be seen.

A search for this planet must be approached with some caution,

(45)

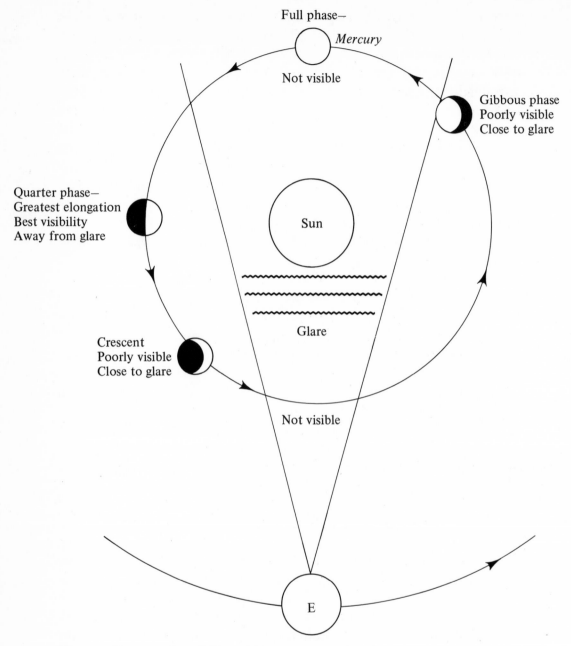

Full phase—
Mercury

Not visible

Gibbous phase
Poorly visible
Close to glare

Quarter phase—
Greatest elongation
Best visibility
Away from glare

Sun

Glare

Crescent
Poorly visible
Close to glare

Not visible

E

Fig. 14: Phases and visibility of Mercury from Earth.

however. *Warning:* look for Mercury only with the unaided eyes, *never* with binoculars or telescope. There is a very real danger of damage to your eyes if the Sun should rise above the horizon while you are searching for the planet with magnifying lenses. Even under the best of circumstances, Mercury is difficult to find because it is a rather dull, yellowish object seen close to the horizon, seldom brighter than a moderately bright star. During some months it may be found just above the horizon in the west immediately after sunset; at other times it is present just above the horizon in the east an hour or so before sunrise. Mercury is so dim that it can easily be overlooked unless the air is very clear and you search for it very carefully; and if your area is affected by sky glow, smog, or atmospheric haze, you may well not be able to find Mercury at all.

According to legend, the great astronomer Copernicus was never able to observe Mercury because of the morning and evening mists in the Polish river valley where he lived. On the other hand, if you live in a desert area with dry, clean air and broad, flat horizons, you may be able to follow the movements of Mercury surprisingly well as it bobs above the horizon on first one side of the Sun and then the other. Don't be misled, however, by a much brighter object that you may see higher in the sky in the evening after sunset or in the morning before sunrise. If it is a bright silvery-white, it is most likely the planet Venus and not Mercury that you are observing.

VENUS. Aside from the moon itself, there is no other object in the heavens more impressively beautiful than the silvery planet Venus, visible high in the western sky for several hours after sunset, or in the eastern sky several hours before sunrise during appropriate viewing times. Whether Venus is playing the role of morning star or evening star, it is unmistakable, sometimes shining so brilliantly that it casts a shadow. As with Mercury, we must look for Venus at the times of its elongations — that is, the times when it is as far to the east or the west of the Sun as it moves in its orbit, since the planet is hidden by the Sun's glare the rest of the time. However, the orbit of Venus around the Sun is much larger than Mercury's, so the planet takes 225 of our days to make one complete circuit. It is also far enough away from the Sun — an average of about sixty-seven million miles compared to Earth's average distance of ninety-three million miles — that it will remain visible in the sky for months at a time at either elongation or before gradually disappearing into the glare in back or in front of the Sun. If you follow its motion day after day, you will be able to see it, as the evening star, gradually setting sooner and sooner after sunset on succeeding days until it can no longer be seen. When it is the morning star, it will rise later and later before sunrise until it can no longer be observed in the growing brightness of dawn.

Fortunately, Venus is far enough away from the Sun at its greatest elongations, and appears high enough above the horizon before dawn or after sunset, that you can safely use binoculars or a telescope to watch it. With a good pair of binoculars you will see that Venus always appears "in phase" — much like a tiny moon. We never see the full disk of the planet during an ordinary night-time viewing. Since Venus shines only by reflected sunlight, we could see the full face of the planet illuminated only when it was on the far side of the Sun from the Earth, a time when it is hidden in the Sun's glare and can only be observed by professional astronomers during daylight hours using special instruments. By the time it reaches a point that it can be seen at night, it is partway around the Sun, and thus you will see only a gibbous phase of the disk illuminated, at most. It is far brighter in the heavens and appears much larger, however, when it is closest to the Earth in its orbit, so that only a quarter phase of the disk can be seen.

MARS, JUPITER, AND SATURN. These planets are all farther from the Sun than the Earth, and we see them best when the Sun is behind us and the full planetary disks are reflecting the sunlight. Because these planets have much larger orbits than the Earth's, they are visible in the sky for longer at a time than the innermost planets and seem to move much more slowly against the background of stars. They are also visible high in the sky away from the vicinity of the Sun, so that observing them presents fewer problems. However, the ease and clarity with which they can be seen depends upon where these planets are located in the solar system with respect to the Earth and the Sun at any given time. At certain times, they may appear so bright and clear that their presence is unmistakable, while at other times they appear so dim and unimpressive that you must know exactly where to look for them to find them at all. At still other times, they vanish from the sky altogether for long periods of time.

Mars, for example, takes almost two years to make its complete orbit around the Sun compared to the Earth's 365¼ days. This means that the Earth is continually "catching up" with Mars, passing it, and moving on around to the other side of the Sun from it. When the two planets are on opposite sides of the Sun in their orbits, they are separated by some 230 million miles or more, and Mars will be invisible to the backyard astronomer because at that time it would be hidden in the Sun's glare. But when the Earth has "caught up" to Mars's slower motion around the Sun, and has come into a direct line between Mars and the Sun — a position known as *opposition* — the distance between the two planets is only a matter of thirty-five to forty-five million miles, and Mars is clearly visible in the night sky (see Fig. 15).

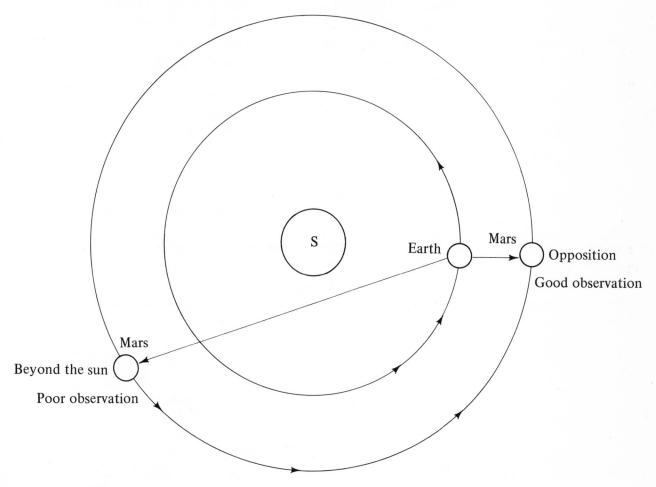

Fig. 15: Mars in opposition.

Because of these solar system mechanics, Mars reaches a favorable point for observation approximately every two and a half years. If the orbits of both the Earth and Mars were perfectly circular, these planets would always be the same distance apart during an opposition, a distance of some forty million miles. But since the orbits of both planets are not circles but ellipses — slightly oval-shaped paths through space — there are times when the Earth passes Mars much closer than at other times. Occasionally the two planets pass as closely as thirty-five million miles. Astronomers studying the planets look forward to such "favorable oppositions," since they provide the best possible opportunity for telescopic study of Mars. Such oppositions are also the choice times to send space probes to the planet. For the amateur astronomer, however, any opposition offers a good chance to study Mars and follow its pattern of motion in the sky, either with the unaided eye or with a telescope. During favorable oppositions, the planet appears a striking orange-red color, brighter than any star, and thus calls attention to itself in the heavens for months at a time.

Both Jupiter and Saturn are also best observed during periods of opposition, but both are so far from the Sun that they take many years to make a complete orbit and therefore remain visible in the sky season after season and year after year. Of the two, however, Jupiter is much the closer and the larger. During opposition it will appear as the fourth brightest object in the nighttime sky, only slightly dimmer and more yellow in color than the planet Venus. Saturn is not so striking to the unaided eye and will be somewhat harder to locate and identify. Even so, it still outshines many prominent stars, and once you have spotted it you can readily follow its slow, stately "wandering" against the fixed background of stars week by week and month by month.

Probably there is no better way for the backyard astronomer to develop a feeling for the vast immensity of the solar system than by following the movements of these five planets through the night sky for a period of time. The outer planets Uranus, Neptune, and Pluto (as well as the tiny planetoids of the Asteroid Belt that lie between Mars and Jupiter) require special telescopic and photographic instruments for location and identification. Once again, it should be said that no telescope should be used in searching for Mercury because of the danger of Sun damage to the eyes. Yet four of the five classical planets — Venus, Mars, Jupiter, and Saturn — can not only be followed and studied with the unaided eye, but also present extraordinary opportunities for telescopic study as well, as we shall see in a later chapter.

● *Vagabonds of the Sky*
There is yet another kind of solar system wanderer that occasionally provides a spectacular display for study with the unaided eye or with binoculars. Comets entering the night sky have drawn the attention of stargazers since time immemorial, and like other unusual celestial events, the appearance of a major comet was once believed to signify impending disaster. It is hardly surprising that ancient stargazers regarded them with wonder and awe, for these mysterious and sometimes erratic vagabonds of the solar system present an appearance unlike anything else to be seen in the heavens.

What exactly are comets? Impressive as they appear, astronomers believe they are actually nothing but small gatherings of space debris — dust, rock chips, ice crystals, and gas — which have gathered together in the vast areas between the planets and then have begun moving, under the influence of the gravitational attraction of various planets and the Sun, in long, cigar-shaped, oval orbits, swinging in very close to the Sun at perihelion and then flying far, far out into the distant reaches of the solar system at aphelion (see Fig. 16).

No one really knows where these balls of "space junk" come from; astronomers sometimes describe them as huge, "dirty snowballs," perhaps no more than a mile or two in diameter when they are traveling through space in the frozen reaches far from the Sun. Nor does anyone understand precisely how certain of the planets maintain such a dominating gravitational control over the movement of comets, but apparently they do. One family of some thirty comets, for example, all have their aphelia in the vicinity of the orbit of mighty Jupiter. Another group moves farther out to the orbit of Saturn, while others have been identified clearly with Uranus or Neptune.

All comets, however, present the same odd pattern of behavior as they travel in their orbits in toward the Sun. In the cold outer reaches of the solar system, a typical comet is nothing more than

(51)

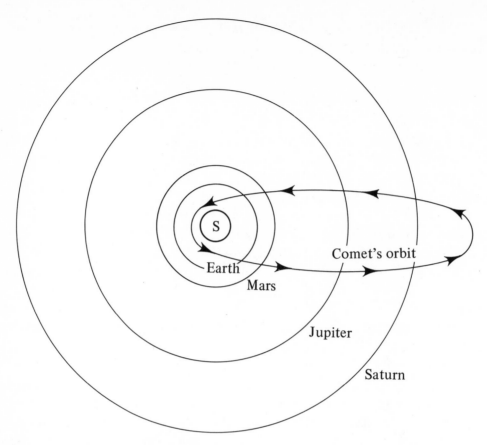

Fig. 16: The cigar-shaped orbit of a comet.

a dark, solid, frozen mass of matter, but as it moves in closer to the Sun it begins to melt and vaporize or sublimate. Bit by bit the solid matter of its nucleus becomes an expanding ball of gas and debris which begins to shine in the Sun's light. As the comet approaches still closer to the Sun, this tenuous ball of gas and dust continues to expand to a diameter of thousands or hundreds of thousands of miles, and a vast streamer of gases begins to trail off to form a luminous "tail" which may string out for millions of miles across space, often easily visible to the unaided eye of observers on Earth (see Fig. 17). The gaseous material forming this luminous tail is so extremely tenuous that the pressure of the light and solar particles thrown out from the Sun tend to push the tail away from the head of the comet so that the comet's tail is always pointing away from the Sun. As the comet approaches the Sun

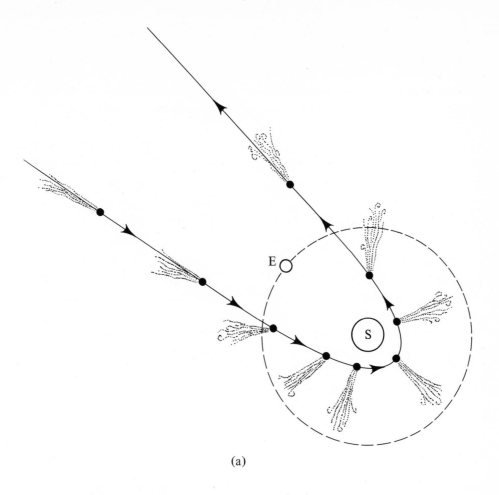

(a)

Parts of a comet

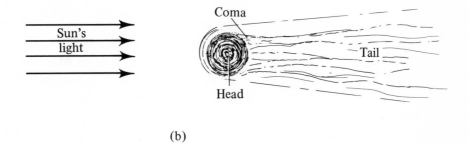

Sun's
light

Coma

Tail

Head

(b)

*Fig. 17: The orbit of a typical comet
around the Sun. Note direction of comet's tail.*

from outer space, the tail seems to trail after the head, but when the comet has rounded the Sun and is moving back into space again, the tail goes first!

Although many comets move in closed orbits and therefore return to swing around the Sun again and again, others appear to travel in an open curve so that once they have swung past the Sun, they move off and out of the solar system altogether, never again to return. Of those with closed orbits, a great many appear with predictable regularity at intervals of years, decades, or centuries. Most famous of all is Halley's Comet, named for Sir Edmund Halley, the Astronomer Royal of England during the early 1700s. When this great comet appeared in the sky in 1682, Halley calculated its orbit, consulting with Sir Isaac Newton, a contemporary and friend. It seemed to Halley that this huge and spectacular comet moved in much the same fashion as a comet that had been previously recorded in 1607 and even earlier in 1531; indeed, there were records of a great comet that had appeared to observers in England in the year 1066, and still other records of sightings that went back before the time of Christ. Halley suspected that all of these sightings were, in truth, of the same great comet which returned in its orbit around the Sun every seventy-five to seventy-six years. He predicted that it would return again to be seen in 1758.

Sure enough, Halley's comet returned within a month of the time that Halley had predicted, although he did not live to see it. It was back again, visible in the sky, at the time of the birth of the American author Mark Twain in 1835, and was visible again on the night of his death in 1910. Today we know that the outermost reaches of the orbit of Halley's Comet lie far beyond the orbit of Neptune, a point the great comet reached in the year 1948 before starting on its return in toward the Sun. Presently, the comet is traveling somewhere between the orbits of Neptune and Uranus, and will once again cross the orbit of the Earth and become visible in our skies sometime in 1985 or 1986.

Few comets are as reliable or spectacular as Halley's Comet. Many appear as little more than tiny fuzzy patches in the sky to the unaided eye and can be seen well only with a small telescope. Many of these "telescopic comets" have regular periods, however, and thus can be spotted by a diligent observer at predictable times.

One, known as Encke's Comet, has a period of three years and can be seen quite well with a small telescope. Its approach is announced in the astronomical atlases and star watchers' guides. A few comets that have recently been visible to the unaided eye are thought to have been nonperiodic comets, following a path around the Sun with such a wide curve that they are believed to have gone on out into space, never to return, or perhaps only to return after hundreds of thousands of years. The Arend-Roland Comet, for example, appeared in April of 1957 and was readily observed with the unaided eye for a short period of time. Mrkos Comet was seen in August of the same year, and Burnham's Comet appeared in the sky in 1960. All three of these are believed to be nonperiodic comets.

Each year, however, a few new or previously unidentified comets are discovered, some visible to the unaided eye, some observable only by telescope. No one knows for sure whether these are newly formed comets appearing for the first time or whether they are older comets that have simply never been previously recorded. Even long-familiar comets have been known to do strange things. In 1858 the extremely bright Donati's Comet appeared with not one but two brilliantly curving tails; that comet has such a huge orbit that it is not expected to return to the vicinity of the Earth again for at least nineteen hundred years, if ever. Another famous one, Biela's Comet, was probably first observed in 1772 and was definitely seen in 1805 and 1826. It continued to return every six or seven years until 1846. Then in that year it was seen to break in two in the sky before observers' eyes and has since disappeared altogether.

Indeed, if there is one thing certain about comets, it is that they are uncertain travelers in the solar system. If some return again and again according to astronomers' calculations, others divide, develop new tails, grow brighter or fainter, or disintegrate and disappear altogether. And just as some vanish, new ones undoubtedly form, although no one is entirely sure where, why, or under what circumstances this happens. Frequently, however, these newly appearing comets are first identified by amateur astronomers. One young amateur comet watcher, Kaoru Ikeya of Japan, has discovered a number of new comets in recent years with a telescope that he built himself, including the famous Ikeya-Seki Comet first seen in 1965.

● *Meteors and Meteorites*

What happens when a recurring or periodic comet breaks up or disintegrates in space? It vanishes from sight, never to be seen again, but it also leaves behind it a vast expanding wake of tenuous gas, dust particles, and small rocks, all of which continue wandering through space. We know this is so because the Earth in its orbit around the Sun occasionally passes through the path of such a disintegrated comet. When it does, the backyard astronomer is treated to another sort of display of celestial fireworks: a meteor shower.

Everyone has seen "shooting stars" in the sky from time to time. Almost any dark night of the year you will see at least a few streak swiftly across the sky and then disappear like the spark from a skyrocket. These "shooting stars" are, of course, nothing of the sort; bright as they may appear, they are seldom more than tiny sand grains or dust particles entering Earth's atmosphere at high accelerations. Most people assume that these particles, known as meteors, must be very large in order to cause such a bright streak across the sky — but in fact the average meteor is probably less than one-eighth inch in diameter.

We know that "empty" space in our solar system is really peppered with such minute particles of matter, all traveling around the Sun in orbits much the same as planets or comets. When such a meteor comes on collision course with the Earth while moving in the right direction, it can enter the upper layers of Earth's atmosphere at speeds as high as 40 miles per second or more — 150,000 miles per hour! At such speeds, the meteor begins banging into air molecules which become thicker and thicker the closer it travels to the Earth's surface. Swiftly the meteor particle is heated up by friction caused by rubbing against air molecules at such an acceleration. Finally, it heats to incandescence and traces a fiery line across the sky. Usually it is totally vaporized long before it reaches the ground.

Some meteors are "lone wolves" traveling the solar system by themselves, while others, usually from disintegrated comets, travel in swarms. The "lone wolves" are often tiny particles made of nickel, iron, or even of stone which may, in many cases, actually be tiny asteroids — members of the huge cluster of debris that moves in a vast orbit around the Sun between Mars and Jupiter.

(56)

We know that all the asteroids do not remain in the Asteroid Belt; some have very eccentric orbits, moving in close to the Sun at perihelion and far out beyond the orbit of Jupiter at aphelion. Once in a rare while, such a mini-asteroid meteor entering the Earth's atmosphere will be large enough so that part of it survives the complete drop to Earth. When this happens, the part that strikes the ground is known as a meteorite, and many have been found and collected by science museums.

On very rare occasions a truly huge meteorite will come down. On June 30, 1908, such a meteorite, probably weighing several hundred tons, crashed into the Earth in northern Siberia. The shock wave was detected up to five hundred miles away, and trees were knocked flat for forty miles in all directions. Some fifty thousand years ago an even larger meteorite struck the ground in central Arizona, leaving a crater that today measures over 4000 feet across and 570 feet deep. Other huge meteorite craters are known in Canada, Oregon, Algeria, and other parts of the world. Fortunately, such meteorite crashes are exceedingly uncommon; if the Siberian meteorite had struck Manhattan Island instead of Siberia, it would have totally demolished all of New York City and much of metropolitan New Jersey in a single blow.

Most meteors disintegrate and vaporize fifty or sixty miles above the Earth's surface, resulting in nothing more than a harmless and beautiful spectacle. Aside from the "lone wolf" meteors that are constantly entering Earth's atmosphere one by one, the Earth meets a number of meteor swarms every year in its orbit around the Sun. When this happens, the observer sees a "meteor shower," a display so striking that the sky may seem to be filled with flying sparks. Many of these meteor swarms are in such reliable orbits that we can predict in advance when the meteor showers will occur each year. Since these meteor showers appear to the Earth observer to radiate from a given point in the sky, the more important showers are named according to the constellations in which they seem to originate, even though they actually have nothing to do with the stars.

On the night of August 12 each year, for example, there is a particularly extensive shower of meteors which seems to originate in the constellation Perseus. This so-called Perseid meteor shower, which goes on all night, provides one of the most reliable and spectacular of all such displays, with meteors appearing as often as every second or two. Other important recurring meteor showers include the Orionid shower which appears to originate in Orion, seen on October 22; the Lyrid shower (from Lyra) on April 21; the Leonid shower, from Leo, on November 17; and the Geminid shower, from Gemini, on December 12. You will not see all of these showers every year, however, since the Earth on some occasions passes through the meteor swarms when North America is in daylight, but current seasonal star watchers' guides will alert you when a given shower is to be visible at night.

In watching such a shower, the best time to observe is between midnight and dawn, since the meteors will then appear about twice as abundantly as earlier in the evening. The reason is that early in the evening we are on the "back side" of the Earth as it moves in its orbit, so that meteors entering the Earth's atmosphere then are "catching up" with us and thus move much more slowly and are less likely to be heated to incandescence. In the early-morning hours, the Earth is turned so that we are on the "front side," and meteors are meeting us head on, entering the atmosphere at higher relative speeds and thus more likely to burn spectacularly.

Meteor showers vary in brilliance from year to year. One of the most brilliant in all history took place on November 13, 1833, when the Earth passed through a particularly thick portion of the Leonid meteor swarm. The greatest display so far in the present century occurred in October of 1946 in a meteor shower connected with the comet Giacobini-Zinner. But even minor meteor showers offer fascinating displays for the backyard astronomer several times a year.

● *Artificial Satellites*

What about man-made objects — artificial satellites or space debris — which can occasionally be seen passing in a slow, stately arc across the sky at night? Since Soviet Russia launched the first Sputnik in 1957, literally thousands of satellite instruments and pieces of launching hardware have been thrown into orbit around the Earth, many of them far enough out that they will continue orbiting for centuries.

Most of these objects are too tiny to be seen with the unaided eye and would be picked up only by the rarest chance with binoculars or a telescope. But some, like the Echo satellites launched by the United States, are extremely bright and readily call attention to themselves as they pass across the sky. Occasionally an artificial satellite will appear to flicker or blink as it travels. This usually occurs when the object is toppling end over end in its orbit so that the Sun is first reflected from the broad side and then from the end. Those experienced in satellite tracking and star watching can obtain prior information about the probable passage of certain artificial satellites from the major professional astronomical handbooks, but for most amateurs the observation of an artificial satellite is a matter of chance — the sort of occasional memorable sight that makes backyard astronomy such a fascinating hobby even for those who have not yet become expert at it.

4

STAR
WATCHING
WITH
BINOCULARS

Throughout thousands of years, the ancient stargazers learned an amazing amount about the Sun, the moon, the solar system, and the distant stars, using no other instruments than their own un-aided vision. With the introduction of magnifying instruments in the early 1600s, however, the horizons of astronomy were pushed back dramatically and the real Age of Astronomical Discovery began. Even the simplest of magnifying instruments had their place in the swift growth of astronomical knowledge, and today the amateur backyard astronomer can expand the horizon of his stargazing immeasurably with the use of an ordinary pair of binoculars.

● *Which Binoculars to Use?*
One important advantage of binocular observation is that an ade-quate pair of binoculars for stargazing is fairly easy to come by. Most families have a pair tucked away somewhere, often on a shelf gathering dust. If you have no binoculars at home, a pair can be purchased at a reasonable price, either new from a reput-

able dealer in cameras and optical instruments or from a second-hand dealer. Secondhand binoculars will serve just as well as a brand-new pair provided that the lenses are clean and the focusing mechanism is unimpaired. Be sure to check out used binoculars very carefully before you buy them, testing them both in daylight and at night to make sure they will bring distant objects into clear, single-image focus. If you have any doubts, have a reputable optical supply house check the lenses and focusing mechanism before you purchase. Sometimes used binoculars will be sold simply because they have become slightly out of adjustment, and can be readily and inexpensively adjusted, but others may be damaged beyond repair. Be sure before you buy.

In addition, make certain the binoculars will be large enough and powerful enough for your purposes. Small opera glasses or toy binoculars will be of little use. You will want a pair of 7 x 35 mm. binoculars, at the least, with a smoothly operating focusing mechanism. 10 x 40 mm. or 10 x 50 mm. binoculars will be even better. Good binoculars should, when in focus, provide a single, clear, in-depth image of distant objects, and should hold their focus when moved about or adjusted for eye width. Many inexpensive binoculars may have some *chromatic aberration* — a distortion of the light that causes a rainbow-colored ring around the field of vision — but for your purposes this will make little difference.

Be sure the lenses are immaculately clean; silicone-treated eyeglass tissues may be used to polish both the large light-gathering lenses and the tiny eyepiece lenses. Unless you really know *exactly* how your binoculars are constructed, don't attempt to unscrew the eyepieces for cleaning, or otherwise tamper with the lens system. If there is dirt, grease, or haze on the inside of the eyepieces or light-gathering lenses, take the instrument to an optical supply house or camera repair shop and have them expertly cleaned.

● *Using Binoculars Effectively*

When you first attempt to use your binoculars for stargazing, you will immediately encounter two difficulties. The first is a problem of focus. It can be extremely difficult to bring binoculars to a proper focus at night, in the dark, unless they have been focused in advance and the focusing mechanism then left undisturbed.

Second, if binoculars are hand-held, there will always be a certain amount of vibration, so that the object being viewed will "flutter" in the field of vision and cannot be studied closely. This problem becomes worse as your arms grow tired from holding the glasses in position for viewing.

Both problems can readily be solved. Before taking the binoculars out on a starry night to study the sky, set the focus under good conditions of visibility during daylight so that only the most minor adjustment is necessary at night. Although celestial objects are vastly farther away than test objects you may use for focusing during the daytime, for practical purposes they require exactly the same focus with binoculars: the focus set at infinity. During daylight, pick a distant object, several miles away if possible, upon which to focus your binoculars and take care that individual eye adjustments, if they are available on your binoculars, are set for clear stereoscopic vision. Once this focus is set, leave it strictly alone until you begin your nighttime viewing. Then, using the moon as a test object, make any fine focus adjustment necessary to bring the detail on the moon's surface into sharp focus. (The sharp contrast of a quarter moon or the line between darkness and light on the surface of a gibbous moon will serve better for this purpose than the comparatively poor-contrast face of a full moon.)

Once you have set the focus in this fashion, it should be exactly right for any other astronomical observation; take care not to alter or tamper with the adjustment. If your binoculars tend to get out of adjustment easily, you may want to make a tiny pin scratch at the exact point of perfect focus adjustment so that you can easily restore the focus if it is inadvertently lost. If possible, reserve the binoculars you use for star observation for this purpose alone so that the focus and adjustment can be left as they are. Then the binoculars will be ready for use at any time.

The problem of proper support for the binoculars can be overcome with a little simple carpentry. No matter how steady your hand may be, you will not be able to hold the glasses adequately still for more than very brief periods of observation without some kind of solid support. A simple portable supporting rig can be built, however, from a long piece of broom handle, one-inch dowel, or two by two inch board cut to convenient length for the observer's height. To one end of this long support piece, nail or screw a small two-inch by four-inch wooden platform made of half-inch plywood, as shown in Figure 18. Then glue a quarter-inch thick-

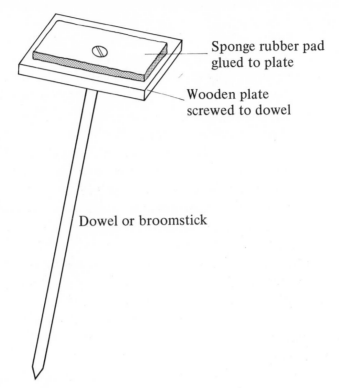

Sponge rubber pad glued to plate

Wooden plate screwed to dowel

Dowel or broomstick

Fig. 18: A wooden support for binoculars.

ness of sponge rubber or polyurethane foam padding to the top of the platform. This device can then be used as a support for the binoculars. It can be tilted to virtually any angle you may desire for viewing, yet will form a solid rest for the glasses and will minimize the amount of vibration. If you wish, the binoculars can be taped onto the supporting plate for even firmer positioning and ease of handling. With a little experimentation while viewing, you will learn to use the glasses at almost any angle without fatigue, and your field of vision will be clear, sharp, and motionless.

Binoculars can be used to study the planets, star clusters, nebulae, and a wide variety of other celestial objects, but their greatest usefulness is to enable the backyard astronomer to become thoroughly familiar with the most beautiful and endlessly varied celestial object to be seen anywhere in the sky: the small dead planet that is Earth's constant companion in its orbit around the Sun — the moon.

● *The Moon and Its Phases*

How often have you looked up at the moon at night? Certainly the sight is familiar — yet if you were to take pencil and paper and try to sketch even a few of the surface markings without looking to refresh your memory, you would probably not do too well. Commonplace as it may be in our lives, the fact is that most people have never really *seen* the moon at all.

Yet if you spend a little time studying the moon through your binoculars, a whole new world will come alive before your eyes. At the point where the bright, illuminated side of the moon dissolves into shadow (a line astronomers call the *terminator*), you can see the tiny jagged teeth of mountain ranges. The great round craters look high at the edges and low and flat in the center, just as we know they are from the moon photographs and astronauts' landings. As you watch the moon slowly changing from one phase to another through your binoculars, you will begin to realize, perhaps for the first time, that this really is another world with a ragged, irregular surface on which a truly incredible amount of detail can be distinguished.

Indeed, you may be discouraged at first because there is *so much* detail visible on the moon's surface. Just as it is easy to be overwhelmed by the vast starry sky until you have become familiar with certain guideposts to help you find your way around, so you can be overwhelmed by the detail on the moon's surface — until you have learned to recognize some of the familiar landmarks. Once you have achieved that, however, each new detail that you observe begins to fall into place until, with a minimum of time and effort spent learning the major landmarks, you will soon find the moon's surface a familiar and fascinating place to spend many enjoyable hours exploring.

Binoculars are the ideal instrument to use for this kind of orientation to the moon. They magnify the surface enough to bring out the major identifying landmarks without bringing out so much detail at once that you are lost trying to identify what you see. What is more, the moon lends itself splendidly to this kind of study because of its unique position as a satellite of our own planet. The moon's diameter is approximately one-fourth that of the Earth, and it travels in orbit around the Earth at a distance of just under a quarter of a million miles. (By comparison Venus, the closest planet to the Earth, never passes nearer than about twenty-six million miles away.) Since the moon makes a complete orbit around the Earth in slightly over 27 days, and since it turns on its own axis in exactly the same interval, the same face is turned toward the Earth at all times. But because it wobbles slightly as it travels in its orbit, somewhat like a slightly out-of-balance top, almost three-fifths of the moon's surface is visible to us at one time or another.

This means that once you have identified a landmark on the moon's surface, you will always be able to find it again any time that portion of the moon's surface is illuminated. With a little study, the major landmarks on the moon can become as familiar as the details of a painting on the wall. But all of the moon's surface cannot be studied adequately at the same time, nor can every feature be seen on every clear night. For one thing, during part of each cycle, the moon is above the horizon during the day and has set during nighttime hours. Even when the moon is in the sky at night, it cannot always be well observed because of the moon's phases. We know that all of the light from the moon is sunlight reflected to Earth from the moon's surface. When the Earth is between the Sun and the moon, the entire face of the moon is illuminated as in Figure 19.

The full moon is not, however, the choice time to distinguish detail on the moon's surface; at such a time the light is striking the moon's surface from directly overhead, like sunlight at noon on a desert in midsummer, so that the surface we see appears flat and shadowless. Then as the moon moves in its orbit around the Earth, sunlight strikes it at more and more of an angle, and part of the surface facing the Earth falls into darkness. At the terminator line where daylight and darkness meet on the moon's surface, you will have the best opportunity to observe craters, plains, and towering mountain ranges in sharp shadowy contrast. A first-quarter or last-quarter moon is perhaps best of all, when illuminated tops of mountain ranges can be seen through binoculars like jagged teeth, while the bases of the same mountains are in shadow

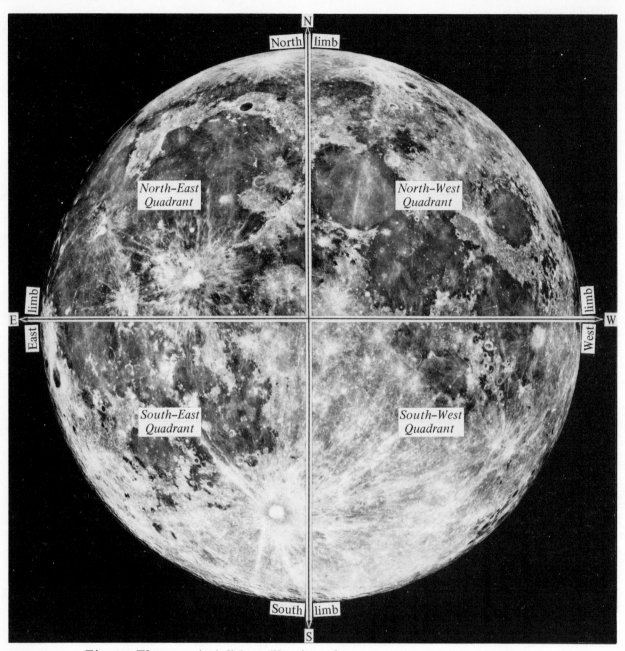

Fig. 19: The moon in full face, illuminated by the Sun, showing individual quadrants.

due to the sharp angle of the light. But at the time of the new moon, the moon has moved around directly between Earth and the Sun so that little or none of the moon's surface is illuminated and nothing can be seen even if the moon is above the horizon during nighttime hours.

Thus to study the moon's surface to best advantage, you will want to watch it in its changing phases from night to night. By following the terminator line as it moves slowly across the moon's surface night by night, you will be able to see the sharp contrast of light and shadow, make out the true contour of surface features, and see detail that cannot be seen any other way. And soon you will be able to fit together the surface details like pieces of a jigsaw puzzle, using certain landmark details as fixed reference points in exploring the moon's surface.

● *Lunar Features*

What kind of details can you see on the moon's surface with binoculars? Some of the terms that are commonly used are misleading. Early astronomers imagined the moon as a living planet like the Earth, complete with seas, oceans, lakes, highlands or swamps, and named various surface landmarks accordingly. Today we know that the moon is a dead and airless world without evidence of any surface water whatever and no sign of life, past or present. Nevertheless, we still use the ancient and romantic names for many of the landmarks with which you will become familiar. Certain kinds of major features in particular will be identifiable with your binoculars:

MARIA (singular *mare*, Latin for "sea"). These are large dark plains scattered hither and yon over the visible surface of the moon, some of them several hundred miles across. These comparatively featureless areas are made up of flat or undulating land with relatively few of the "pockmarks" or meteorite impact craters that are so profusely scattered over other parts of the moon. Scientists speculate that the maria may have been formed by the flow of molten rock over vast areas following impacts by monstrous meteorites eons ago. The craters that are found here and there on the surface of the maria are believed to have been formed more recently. Characteristically, the maria present a rather gray, smooth appearance in sharp contrast to the lighter, brownish-white areas of mountains and multiple craters. Mistaken for vast oceans by early astronomers, the maria constitute important landmarks on the moon's surface, and many of them bear distinctive names. Other similar areas are referred to as "oceans," "marshes," and "lagoons."

MOUNTAIN RANGES. Many of the maria are surrounded by distinct linear mountain ranges, much like earthly mountains, with peaks which reach high above the floor of the plain — in some cases as much as 30,000 feet. Several easily distinguishable mountain ranges are important landmarks in finding our way about the moon's surface.

CRATERS. These are the most impressive features of the entire moon surface, occurring literally by the millions, scattered thickly in some areas, more sparsely in others. These distinctive "pockmarks" range in size from tiny pits a few inches in diameter to craters so huge — ranging from 45 to 150 miles in diameter — that they are sometimes called "ringwalls" or "ring plains." Astronomers are convinced that virtually all of these "pockmarks" are meteorite-impact craters — scars resulting from huge meteorites that have crashed into the rocky surface of the moon. Typically, the craters have high, rugged walls that slope outward onto the surrounding plains, but which fall steeply inward into central flattened basins.

Many craters have central peaks, sometimes rising thousands of feet from the floor of the interior basin. One famous crater, Copernicus, has seven such peaks in the middle of its ring plain. Possibly volcanic action also helped in the formation of some of the craters; certainly the central basins of some of them appear to have been filled with molten rock at some time in the past. But there is evidence that these meteorite-impact craters were formed one at a time over many, many thousands of years and still are forming even today. We know this because many of the craters show evidence of great age, with marked breakdown and erosion of the rims, while others appear comparatively "young" and fresh, and in some cases there are impact craters on top of impact craters — fresh craters that are actually superimposed on the rim of older craters.

RAY SYSTEMS. Certain of the huge craters on the moon's surface display an additional feature so prominent that it can be seen with the naked eye and even more clearly with binoculars under certain conditions of light. These are the systems of long, brilliant rays or streaks radiating out from certain of the impact craters, much like spokes from a wheel. Often these ray systems appear brilliantly white in comparison to darker areas of the moon's surface, and the rays radiating from some craters — Tycho, for example — are as much as seventeen hundred miles long.

No one is certain exactly what these rays are. In some cases they may have been formed by surface dust thrown out by the meteor when it struck to form the crater. Or the rays may be great cracks in the moon's surface caused by the disturbance of the meteorite impact. It is these ray systems, seen by the naked eye, that give the full moon its odd resemblance to a peeled orange, and their true nature is an important matter for investigation for space scientists of the future. For our purposes, they are extremely helpful in identifying certain key craters that are important as landmarks on the moon's surface.

VALLEYS, RIFTS, AND WALLS. In addition to the major features discussed above, there are a number of minor yet fascinating features on the moon's surface which are visible in certain places under ideal lighting conditions. Among these are deep, narrow valleys or canyons that run in straight lines; long linear breaks or rifts in the rock, spoken of as *rills*; and other linear escarpments or walls that seem to rise up suddenly above the surface of the plain below. In the check list of individual identifying features of the moon's surface that follows, we will mention a few of these surface curiosities that are particularly well known. You may find them harder to identify than some of the other major features, but occasionally when lighting conditions are ideal, you should be able to find them with binoculars if you know where to look.

● *A Check List of Lunar Surface Features*

In order to single out and identify some of the more striking major features of the moon's surface as guideposts, it will be convenient for us to divide the surface of the moon as you see it with your binoculars into four quarters or quadrants as indicated in Figure 20. The upper edge of the disk is north and the bottom edge south as you might expect; the left edge is regarded as east and the right edge west according to astronomical convention. When the moon is viewed through most telescopes, the image is inverted in the telescopic field, and astronomers customarily depict this inverted image in their pictures of the moon, with north to the

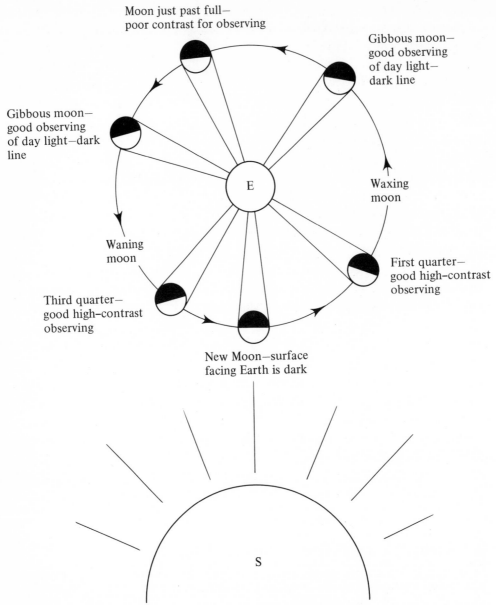

Fig. 20: The moon's phases, as observed from Earth.

bottom edge and south to the top. We will use the more familiar pattern of north to the top, but if you consult moon atlases for more detail later, you may have to turn the atlases upside down for use with binoculars.

Rather than tackle the entire visible surface of the moon willy-nilly, it will be easier to pick out the major landmarks quadrant by quadrant. Remember that the appearance of any given feature may change dramatically from night to night. A particular crater may, for example, be almost invisible with binoculars one night, yet be clearly distinguishable two nights later because of the shifting angle of the light from the Sun, and stand out in stark dramatic black-and-white contrast the following week. It is important to learn not only *where* the highlighted features are to be found, but also to develop a "feel" for the nature of these features in the changing light as the moon waxes and wanes.

THE NORTHWEST QUADRANT. (See Fig. 21.) The most striking features in this quadrant of the moon's surface under any illumination are three huge and easily distinguishable maria or seas: the Mare Crisium (Sea of Crises); the Mare Tranquillitatis (Sea of Tranquillity); and the Mare Serenitatis (Sea of Serenity). To the north, near the midline, is the smaller Mare Frigoris (Sea of Cold). Within the Mare Serenitatis you should be able to identify the crater Bessel and the bright white spot, once thought to be a crater, called Linné. Bordering the Mare Serenitatis near the midline are two mighty mountain ranges, the Haemus Mountains with peaks some eight thousand feet high and the Caucasus Mountains, towering twelve thousand feet above the plain. At the north end of the Caucasus Mountains is a striking highland area, the Alps, with a deep canyon or rift, the Alpine Valley, lying between the Alps and the Mare Frigoris to the north. Close to the western limb are two smaller "seas," the Mare Smythii (Smyth's Sea) and Mare Marginis (Marginal Sea). These two maria can be seen well only at certain times when the moon has wobbled around enough barely to reveal them.

Among the notable craters in this quadrant you will be able to find two prominent pairs. Aristoteles and Eudoxus lie north and south between the Mare Serenitatis and the Mare Frigoris, while Hercules and Atlas lie east and west to the north of the Mare Serenitatis. Julius Caesar is a very dark-floored crater lying just east of the Mare Tranquillitatis. Other striking craters in this quadrant include the huge hundred-mile crater named Gauss which lies on the northwest limb and is best seen when the moon is in the crescent phase, and Scoresby, a small but conspicuous crater near the north pole.

(71)

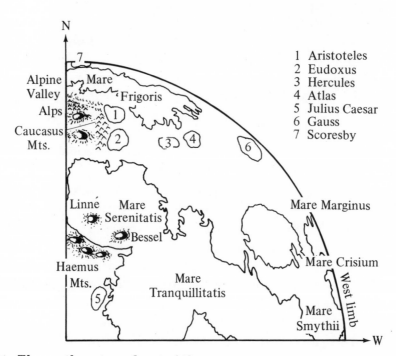

Fig. 21: The northwest quadrant of the moon.

1 Aristoteles
2 Eudoxus
3 Hercules
4 Atlas
5 Julius Caesar
6 Gauss
7 Scoresby

THE SOUTHWEST QUADRANT. (See Fig. 22.) This quadrant is marked by two darkened maria, both of which appear directly connected with the larger Mare Tranquillitatis to the north: the Mare Nectaris (Sea of Nectar) and the larger Mare Fecunditatis (Sea of Fertility). Much of the rest of the quadrant is covered with a ragged, mountainous terrain, including multitudes of large and small craters. Right on the southern rim of the disk are the Leibnitz Mountains which are believed to have the highest peaks on the moon, ranging up to thirty thousand feet.

Among the major craters, Fracastorius is a striking, dark-bottomed ring plain just south of the Mare Nectaris. East of the Mare Nectaris near the midline are two striking craters, Hipparchus and Albategnius, each some eighty miles in diameter, with their ringwalls broken by smaller, newer craters. These gigantic meteorite scars are difficult to identify at the full moon but can be seen clearly at half-moon phase when they lie on the terminator between daylight and dark. Another major crater, Petavius, is located between the southern end of the Mare Fecunditatis and the southwest limb of the disk. Near Petavius and just on the western limb lies the crater Wilhelm Humboldt, a huge ringwall 120 miles across which appears especially clear just after the full moon. In the central part of the disk in the southwest quadrant is a bewildering maze of craters superimposed on craters, as well as such mighty linear mountain ranges as the Altai Mountains which cut across or between the impact craters.

THE NORTHEAST QUADRANT. Although this quadrant of the moon's disk is covered almost completely by the huge Mare Imbrium (Sea of Showers), seven hundred miles across, and the northern half of the less well-defined Oceanus Procellarum (Ocean of Storms), it also contains some of the most striking and easily identified craters on the entire surface of the moon, as well as two major mountain ranges (see Fig. 23). Just south of the Mare Imbrium, and forming its southwestern border, is a huge triangle of ragged peaks, the Appenine Mountains. Still another striking range, the Jura Mountains, can be found along the northern rim of the Mare Imbrium.

The Carpathian Mountains march in a long line across the flatland between the Mare Imbrium and the Oceanus Procellarum. This great range of mountains lies just north of two impressive

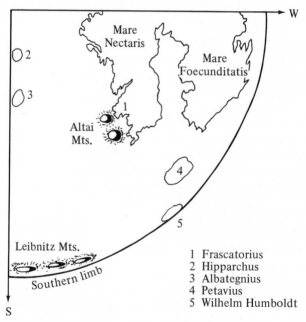

Fig. 22: The southwest quadrant of the moon.

and rather isolated craters: Eratosthenes, which appears sharp-edged and deep when it lies on the terminator, and Copernicus, a huge crater that lies in the center of a bright ray system that is particularly conspicuous at or near full moon. Almost due east of Copernicus in the Oceanus Procellarum is a much smaller crater, Kepler, which is nevertheless almost as striking as Copernicus because it, too, features an intensely bright-colored ray system. A third ray system, the brightest-appearing formation on the entire surface of the moon under certain lighting conditions, surrounds the crater Aristarchus, directly north of Kepler and forming a right-angle triangle with Copernicus and Kepler.

Still another notable crater in this quadrant is Plato, lying between the Mare Imbrium and the Mare Frigoris at the western end of the Jura Mountains. Plato is particularly striking because its central ring plain always appears very dark and smooth. Also easy to identify is the crater Archimedes, lying midway between Plato and the Appenine Mountains and bordering on a particularly smooth area of the Mare Imbrium.

THE SOUTHEAST QUADRANT. (See Fig. 24.) This area of the moon's surface features a wide variety of striking landmarks that most observers will find easy to identify. Two major maria — the easily distinguished Mare Nubium (Sea of Clouds) and the dark-bottomed Mare Humorum (Sea of Humors) — seem to extend southward as branches of the great Oceanus Procellarum to the north. Farther south lies a vast ragged upland area covered with craters of all sizes. Three large ones lie together in a north-to-south direction bordering the Mare Nubium to the west: the ninety-mile Ptolemaeus to the north, Alphonsus in the middle, and Arzachel to the south. Following this line of craters still farther south, you will find another large and striking crater named Purbach. These craters are particularly noticeable at the gibbous phase or half-moon stage, when they fall into sharp relief along the terminator line.

Other craters are equally remarkable. Due east and close to the limb is Grimaldi, which sometimes appears as the darkest spot on the moon. The floor of this 120-mile ring plain appears almost black under most lighting conditions. Far to the south is Clavius, the second largest crater on the moon, measuring some 145 miles across, with crater walls towering as much as 17,000 feet above

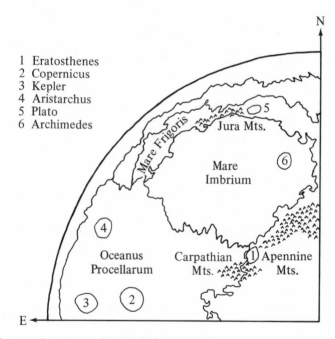

1 Eratosthenes
2 Copernicus
3 Kepler
4 Aristarchus
5 Plato
6 Archimedes

Fig. 23: The northeast quadrant of the moon.

the floor. Clavius is so large that it can easily be distinguished by the naked eye when the daylight-darkness line crosses it, and with binoculars you can identify a whole chain of smaller craters superimposed on it. Halfway between Clavius and the Mare Nubium is a smaller but strikingly brilliant crater, Tycho, which is the center of an extremely bright ray system. Under certain conditions of light, whitish rays streaming out from the walls of this crater can be traced as far as 1700 miles across the moon's surface.

Finally, near the southwest margin of the Mare Nubium, and very close to the crater Purbach, is a famous rift or cleft known as the Straight Wall. This formation appears as a striking white line in some illuminations and is a dark line at other times.

It is obvious from the photographs accompanying our guidepost moon maps that the check list of striking features we have discussed above barely scratches the surface. There are multitudes of other surface details that can be identified with careful binocular searching of the moon during its changing phases. The landmarks we have singled out are intended merely as a starting place, a way that you can open the door to a fascinating and detailed exploration of the surface of this small satellite world at your own speed. You will find much more detailed photographs of the moon, taken in many different phases, together with highly detailed maps and drawings of the major features, in any good moon atlas or atlas of astronomy. But once you have oriented yourself to the features in the check list above, you will have become familiar not only with certain important landmarks themselves, but also with the ever-changing lighting conditions which make the moon's surface such a fascinating and variable place to explore with your binoculars.

With a small telescope, these landmarks will appear even more clearly, and a multitude of others can easily be identified. By investing a little time and effort, the moon's face will soon become thoroughly familiar and provide you with many hours of pleasure and discovery.

● *Following the Planets*
Binoculars will also be helpful in tracing the paths of the planets and observing them. As we mentioned earlier, binoculars should

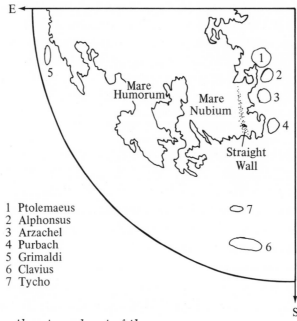

E

S

Mare
Humorum

Mare
Nubium

Straight
Wall

1
2
3
4

5

7

6

1 Ptolemaeus
2 Alphonsus
3 Arzachel
4 Purbach
5 Grimaldi
6 Clavius
7 Tycho

Fig. 24: The southeast quadrant of the moon.

(78)

not be used in searching for Mercury because of the danger of inadvertent exposure to the Sun's rays, but Venus is a different matter. This brilliant planet remains high in the sky long after sunset or long before sunrise, and at such times you can safely use binoculars to observe it. With good support for your binoculars to avoid vibration, you will easily be able to distinguish the changing phases of this planet. You will also be able to see for yourself the remarkable increase in its apparent size as it moves around from the Sun toward the Earth.

It may be surprising to discover that Venus shows the skimpiest of phases — a well-defined last quarter or first quarter — at the time it appears biggest and brightest in the sky, and that it becomes notably smaller and less brilliant as it passes from first quarter to gibbous phase while traveling in its orbit around the Sun. At any time that it is visible in the sky, however, you will be able to see beyond question that Venus presents a distinct disk, even though part of it lies in shadow, and not the mere pinpoint of light demonstrated even by the largest and brightest stars.

Mars, Jupiter, and Saturn can also be followed in their wandering across the sky once you have identified and located them. At favorable oppositions, Mars and Jupiter will both appear as small but distinct disks through binoculars, although no surface detail can be distinguished. Mars always appears a distinctive orange-red color, more orange than red when seen through binoculars than with the unaided eye, while Jupiter appears a pale silvery-yellow. When Jupiter is in favorable opposition, closest to the Earth in its orbit, you may be able to distinguish the four tiny pinpoints of light that represent the four largest of Jupiter's twelve satellites. You will also be able to distinguish a distinct difference in the apparent size of Jupiter when it is close to the Earth and when it is moving far away from the Earth in its orbit around the Sun.

Saturn is more difficult to find, and you will need timely star maps to help you locate it. At best you will find it a rather dim, yellowish point of light in your binoculars, not clearly distinguishable as a disk and with no sign of its spectacular ring system. To observe Saturn's rings, a telescope will be necessary. Nevertheless, it is possible with binoculars to follow the weekly and monthly motion of this distant planet very closely against the background of fixed stars as it makes its stately way in orbit around the Sun.

● *Star Searching with Binoculars*

A good pair of binoculars will provide the backyard astronomer with the most breathtaking surprises, however, in the process of exploring the panoply of stars that lie far beyond our solar system, for there is no better way to discover the richness of the star blanket in the heavens than to compare familiar areas as seen with the unaided eye with the same areas observed through binoculars. There is hardly a constellation in the sky that will not spring out in rich and beautiful detail far beyond anything that can be seen with the unaided eye when it is captured in a binocular field, and every constellation has its special surprises. Here the breadth of the visual field that can be seen with binoculars is a particular advantage. Whereas with a telescope you must aim and focus on a single star or other celestial object, viewing the familiar heavens with binoculars is like viewing a page of fine print with a powerful magnifying glass: each tiny detail appears sharp and clear, the pattern of the constellations can still be seen, and the surprises lie in what can be seen with the binoculars that is virtually invisible to the unaided eye.

We cannot begin to detail here all of the fascinating stellar objects you can find in the heavens with your binoculars. Indeed, much of the fun of sky exploring is to discover for yourself the multitude of strange and varied objects that can be found. It is possible here to suggest only a few of the kinds of celestial objects you will be able to find as you begin exploring on your own.

For a simple example, look at the familiar Big Dipper of Ursa Major, first with the unaided eye and then with binoculars. To the unaided eye the Dipper appears to be made up of seven moderately bright stars, one of which (the star where the handle joins the dipper) appears noticeably dimmer than the others. If you look more closely you will see that Mizar, the next-to-the-last star in the handle, seems to have a small, faint companion very close by — a star named Alcor. You can even distinguish that Mizar and Alcor, besides differing in apparent brightness, are distinctly different colors. Now look at this pair of stars through the binoculars. With the help of this magnification, you will see that Mizar and Alcor are distinctly separate and actually appear quite far apart. What appeared to the unaided eye to be a double or binary star, now is seen to be nothing of the sort. Although these two stars appear close together, they are actually many light-years apart. In fact, through the binoculars you can just distinguish another faint star lying between Mizar and Alcor. But most surprisingly, you will be able to see that Mizar itself *is* a true double star or binary — two tiny pinpoints of light lying extremely close to each other. In fact, Mizar is one of the finest double stars that you will be able to find for observation later with the aid of a small telescope.

Next find the Little Dipper and locate its brightest star, Kochab, located at the lip of the dipper. To the unaided eye, all the stars of the Little Dipper seem quite dim, with Kochab only slightly brighter than the others, and all appear undistinguished in color. Through binoculars, however, Kochab appears clearly orange in color compared to the yellow-white of the other stars in the Little Dipper.

These simple observations illustrate two important properties of any magnifying lens in star searching: the power to *resolve* or separate stars which appear very close together to the unaided eye; and the power to *define* such detail as the colors or positions of stars more clearly. The so-called *resolving power* of your binoculars will be most clearly demonstrated in observing the Milky Way which appears to the unaided eye as a hazy band of fuzzy faint light crossing the sky like a luminous milky river.

Even under good viewing conditions it is difficult to distinguish with the unaided eye any individual pinpoint of light in the Milky Way. But through binoculars the hazy cloud of light is resolved into a dazzling multitude of individual stars, thousands upon millions of them. It is only when we see this great body of stars that makes up our own galaxy that we realize that the stars of the constellations and the individual bright stars we have learned to recognize by name are really close neighbors to our own Sun compared to the multitudes of distant stars in our galaxy. Those tiny pinpoints of light that pepper the Milky Way are shining just as brightly and fiercely in their place in space as Sirius or Vega, but appear to us only as the tiniest and faintest pinpoints of light because of their enormous distances.

The power of binoculars to define hazy or indistinct objects in the sky is splendidly illustrated in another familiar constellation, Orion. Orion's arms and legs are represented by two widespread bright stars above the three stars of his belt and two below. Even to the unaided eye Betelgeuse, the highest of Orion's arms, appears a bright orange color while Rigel, marking his forward foot, can be seen to be a brilliant blue-white. The stars forming Orion's belt are also sharply clear, but the chain of stars hanging down to mark his dagger or sword are not so distinct. To the unaided eye there seem to be three of these stars, although the middle one seems curiously hazy in comparison with the upper and lower ones. Now look at these three "sword stars" through binoculars and you will see quite a different picture. The top "star" of the sword is not really a single star at all but three stars very close together. Through the binoculars, the bottom star of the three can be seen to be a double or binary star. Most interesting of all is the middle of the three sword stars, for with binoculars you will see that this is not a star at all but a hazy cloud which appears like a tiny bit of cotton fluff in the sky.

If you look very closely you will be able to distinguish a number of extremely indistinct pinpoints of light within this hazy area. What you are seeing is, in fact, a great gaseous nebula — a huge cloud of luminous gas which is excited to shining luminosity by a famous multiple star, Theta Orionis, sometimes called the Trapezium, that lies in the midst of the gas cloud. This particular diffuse nebula in the sword of Orion is one of the most famous because it can actually be seen, just barely, with the unaided eye; but without the aid of binoculars it is easy to miss this and to assume that these sword stars are nothing but tiny pinpoints of light instead of the complex structures they really are.

Numerous other distinctive celestial objects can also be identified with binoculars. If you follow the three belt stars of Orion upward to the right as pointers, you will encounter the bright, orange-red star Aldebaran in the constellation Taurus. Follow the same line still farther and you will come to a rather isolated patch of hazy light which, on closer observation, can be seen to be made up of a group of stars, one moderately bright, the others quite dim. This group is known as the Pleiades, sometimes called "The Seven Sisters," and on a particularly clear night you should be able to count seven stars with the unaided eye. Interestingly enough, this group of stars is part of a true "open cluster" of stars, all of which lie comparatively close to each other in space and are not merely a line-of-sight effect.

But when you study the Pleiades with binoculars, you see far more than a few faint stars. The seven brightest will suddenly stand out like blue-white diamonds on a field of black velvet. Even more remarkable, dozens upon dozens of other stars in this cluster will also become visible — far too many to count. It has been estimated that as many as 250 additional stars can be seen in the Pleiades cluster with a good pair of binoculars, and with a small telescope as many as 500 are visible.

A similar open cluster of stars is the Hyades, a group of stars which lie around Aldebaran itself. The Hyades are fainter and more widespread than the Pleiades, and to the unaided eye they appear overpowered by the bright, orange-red light of Aldebaran (which is not actually a member of the cluster at all but simply happens to lie in the same direction). Through binoculars, however, the Hyades appear as a distinct cluster of dim orange stars, sharply in contrast to the highly luminous blue-white stars of the Pleiades. Still another such open cluster that can easily be seen with binoculars is a group called Praesepe, lying on a line between Pollux in the constellation Gemini and bright Regulus in the constellation Leo.

Quite a different sort of star cluster can be seen in the constellation Hercules. First locate the bright orange star Arcturus in Boötes by following the handle stars of the Big Dipper and extending the arc. Beyond and a little above Arcturus you will find the Corona Borealis, the semicircle of stars that form a sort of crown or diadem in the sky. In a direct line drawn from Arcturus through the Corona and extended a little farther, you will come to the irregular constellation Hercules. On a clear dark night, with the unaided eye you can see a faint hazy patch of light in this constellation. With binoculars you will be able to see this object much more clearly; there are no distinct points of starlight within it, but the whole structure looks like a huge fuzzy star.

What you are seeing is, in fact, not a single star at all, nor even a nebula such as the one in Orion's sword (which it greatly resem-

bles through the binoculars) but rather a so-called *globular cluster* of stars made up of multitudes of stars closely packed together.
Such globular clusters are believed to exist by the thousands,
hovering in a huge sphere around the hub of our galaxy rather
like hornets hovering around a nest. With powerful telescopes,
astronomers have been able to determine that the globular cluster
in Hercules consists of multitudes of individual stars, perhaps as
many as half a million, lying within a sphere one hundred light-
years in diameter — a tiny subgalaxy of stars within our own
galaxy.

The Corona Borealis is another constellation which appears far
more brilliant, interesting, and varied with binoculars than to
the unaided eye. Without the binoculars the Corona appears to be
a semicircle of about six stars, two of which are quite bright, the
others dim. Through binoculars you will find two much fainter
stars located in the "bowl" of the crown (see Fig. 25). The one to
the right, known as M Corona Borealis, is not ordinarily visible
to the naked eye but can be seen clearly with binoculars as a faint,
steady star. To the left is R Corona Borealis. This star is particu-

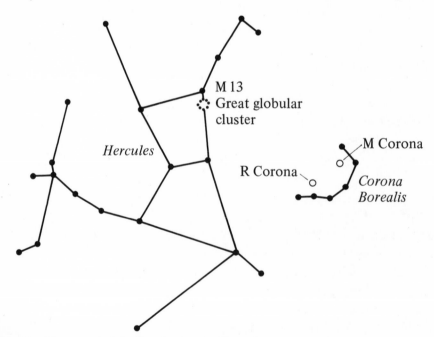

*Fig. 25: The great globular cluster in Hercules,
with M- and R-Corona Borealis.*

(84)

larly interesting to watch from time to time, for it is a fascinating *variable star*. Most of the time it is just on the fringe of visibility to the unaided eye but can be seen quite clearly with binoculars. But at irregular intervals — sometimes as often as every two or three days, sometimes only once a month or even longer — this star will seem to disappear altogether for a brief period, only to reappear as abruptly as it faded.

Unlike many other variable stars, which shift or vary in brightness at regular intervals, R Corona has no predictable period of brightness or dimness, so you can never be sure whether you will see it on a given night or not. But it provides an opportunity, even with binoculars, to follow its brightening or dimming and to see for yourself that certain stars do not shine with the steady brightness of our Sun, but periodically flare and dim with a variability that can easily be observed by the amateur astronomer.

Finally, as one more example of the variety of celestial objects that can be seen with binoculars, locate the polestar and extend a line from it through the center of Cassiopeia and on half again the same distance beyond. This line will then reach the constellation Andromeda, which lies slightly above the square of Pegasus. In Andromeda you will see another misty patch of light which appears to the unaided eye much like the great nebula in Orion's sword. With binoculars, however, you will be able to see that this object is oval-shaped rather than round and that no individual stars are distinguishable. This oval patch is something quite different from anything else we have discussed. Although it looks like a gaseous nebula, it is in fact an entire distant galaxy of stars, the great spiral galaxy in Andromeda. This is one of the nearest of all other galaxies to our own, and is believed to be very similar in size, shape, and appearance to our own galaxy, yet it is incredibly more distant than any other object in the sky — a whole other island universe made up of billions of stars, but lying so far away from us that it appears as an almost insignificant patch of haze in the night sky.

These are only a very few of the multitudes of surprises that are waiting in the sky for the backyard astronomer with a good set of binoculars. Even with such low magnification, the nighttime universe that you can observe is expanded remarkably. Old familiar objects take on a new appearance, while other objects become visible that could not otherwise be seen at all. But once you have become familiar with the skies with the aid of binoculars, you will doubtless begin considering one further step: a more ambitious exploration of the nighttime heavens with a small but serviceable telescope.

5

THE UNIVERSE BY TELESCOPE

Useful as binoculars may be in locating and observing multitudes of celestial objects, any serious backyard astronomer will sooner or later want a telescope to aid him in his exploring. Many people assume, without thinking, that only huge telescopes like those in the great scientific observatories could possibly be effective for studying the sky, and that any useful telescope must necessarily be extremely costly. Fortunately neither of these ideas is true. While professional astronomers do indeed require large telescopes and complicated equipment to probe the outer limits of the universe and to study distant galaxies, the amateur backyard astronomer will find that a small, low-priced telescope of good quality can greatly enrich his study of the nighttime sky and provide many hours of enjoyable observation at relatively little cost.

Surprisingly enough, many of the small and inexpensive instruments available today are at least as good and often vastly superior to the primitive telescopes that Galileo used in making his astronomical discoveries, and may actually enable you to observe things that Galileo's instruments could not have revealed at all. But it is important to have some basic information about the kinds of telescopes, the sizes that are best suited for backyard astronomy, and the kinds of telescope mountings that are necessary before you begin shopping for a telescope for your backyard observatory.

Two different kinds of telescopes are commonly used for astronomical observation, each with certain advantages and certain disadvantages. Perhaps most familiar is the so-called *refractor telescope*, a direct descendant of the earliest telescopes invented in Holland in the early 1600s and later modified by Galileo for his stargazing. The other variety is the *reflector telescope*, first invented by Sir Isaac Newton in order to overcome certain of the disadvantages of refractor telescopes, and a type of instrument that is widely used by amateur astronomers today.

The earliest refractor telescope was little more than a long hollow tube with specially ground glass lenses mounted in either end. One end of the tube held a rather large *objective* or "light-gathering" lens, thin at the edges and bulging outward on either side in a biconvex form. The purpose of this lens was to gather light from the stars and bend the light rays so that they came to a focus at some point down the tube. If a small piece of ground glass or waxed paper were held at this so-called *focal point* of the objective lens, a small inverted image of the distant object would be clearly seen. The second lens, mounted in the other end of the tube near the focal point of the objective lens, was called the *eyepiece* or *ocular* lens and served simply to magnify the image at the focal point so that it appeared larger through the lens than when seen by the unaided eye.

In an early modification of this early "optical tube," the eyepiece or ocular lens was mounted in a separate tube that fit into the end of the tube holding the objective lens (see Fig. 26). This permitted the observer to move the two lenses closer together or farther apart at will. By manipulating the two lenses, it was possible to bring the magnified image of distant objects into a sharp focus for observing.

One great advantage of any refractor telescope is that a comparatively small objective lens no more than two or three inches in diameter has a remarkable light-gathering power, and when used with a very small ocular lens can greatly magnify celestial objects and bring them to a clear and brilliant focus. But early astronomers soon found that refractor telescopes had certain

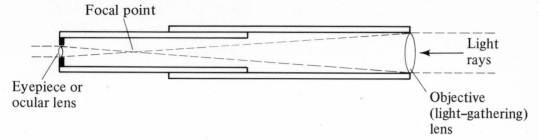

Fig. 26: Principle of the refractor telescope.

built-in disadvantages. One serious problem was that light from celestial objects, in passing through the glass of the objective lens, tended to separate into its component colors so that the image at the focal point seemed to be surrounded by fringes of color, a condition known as *chromatic aberration* (see Fig. 27). In addition, because the objective lens had to be thicker at the center than at the edges, light entering the telescope through the edges of the lens tended to be bent or refracted less than that passing through thicker parts so that the part of the image at the edge of the field

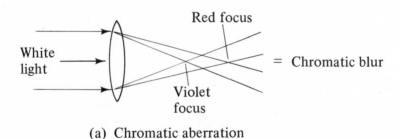

(a) Chromatic aberration

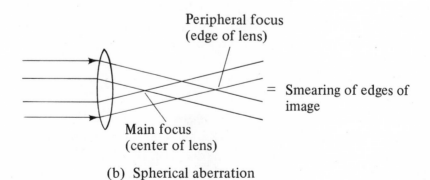

(b) Spherical aberration

Fig. 27: Chromatic and spherical aberrations.

(89)

of vision tended to be slightly distorted or smeared, a condition known as *spherical aberration*.

One way to avoid these problems was to make a very large, thin objective lens that bent the light very little, so that the focal point was a long distance away from the lens. Some early astronomers built refractor telescopes that were dozens or even hundreds of feet long — but these proved to be so clumsy, unwieldy, or unstable that they were very difficult to use. In modern times optical engineers have developed multiple lenses made of different kinds of glass to correct or counteract these problems. Modern refractor telescopes may have as many as six different components making up the objective or eyepiece lenses. But since each of the component lenses must be ground and fitted to a high degree of precision, a really good refractor telescope, even a small one, may be quite expensive.

Even disregarding expense, there is a practical limit to how big or powerful a refractor telescope can be made. The larger the telescope, the heavier and thicker the objective lens must be, and these lenses must be made from virtually flawless glass. Thus a refractor telescope with an objective lens of 5 or 6 inches is extremely expensive to construct, and telescopes with still larger objective lenses require special mounting and balancing devices to hold such a large and heavy piece of glass in place for use. The largest refractor telescope in professional use today, and probably the largest ever likely to be built, is a fine telescope at the Yerkes Observatory outside of Chicago, with an objective lens only forty inches — slightly more than one yard — in diameter.

Because of these early difficulties with refractor telescopes, a totally different type of instrument, the so-called reflector telescope, was invented. These instruments have an enormous advantage over the refractor telescopes because the starlight entering the telescope is not passed through a glass objective lens at all before coming to focus at the eyepiece. Instead it is passed down a completely open-ended tube to strike a curving mirror at the bottom. The mirror's surface is carefully ground to a dish-shaped curve known as a parabola. Parallel light rays striking the parabolic mirror of a reflector telescope then bounce off the mirror at such an angle that they are brought to a focus at a focal point above the mirror (see Fig. 28). In the most common type of reflector telescope, first designed by Sir Isaac Newton, a small flat

Newtonian System (Best for amateur observation)

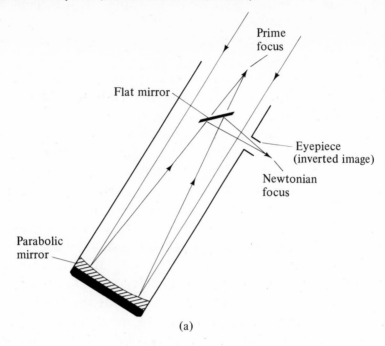

Prime
focus

Flat mirror

Eyepiece
(inverted image)

Newtonian
focus

Parabolic
mirror

(a)

Cassegrain System (For instrumental and photographic work)

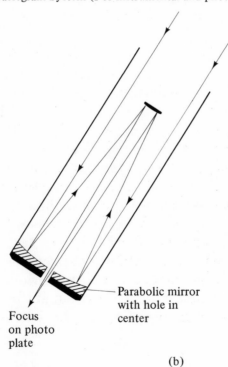

Parabolic mirror
with hole in
center

Focus
on photo
plate

(b)

Fig. 28: Two types of reflector telescopes.

(91)

mirror is suspended diagonally in the tube to intercept the reflected light rays just before they reach their focal point and pass them at a 90-degree angle into a magnifying eyepiece at the side of the telescope tube.

Because the light from the stars never passes through a thick objective lens of glass but is merely reflected by a focusing mirror, the glass of the reflector's mirror need not be perfect; only the curving mirror surface must be ground and polished to precision. This means that comparatively large light-collecting mirrors can be ground at far less cost than objective lenses for refractor telescopes of comparable size. Even more important, there is no chromatic or spherical aberration of light rays, so that the reflected and focused image in the reflector telescope is free of these distortions. And while it is true that a reflecting mirror does not gather as much light as a refracting objective lens of comparable size, it has proved both practical and inexpensive to make reflecting mirrors much larger than refracting lenses. Thus the largest reflector telescope in the world today, the Hale telescope at Mount Palomar Observatory in California, has a parabolic mirror that measures 200 inches (almost 17 feet) in diameter, and a reflector telescope currently under construction in the Soviet Union will have a 250-inch reflecting mirror.

Which kind of telescope is most practical for the beginning amateur astronomer? There are a number of factors you will want to consider. A good refractor telescope, with lens systems to correct chromatic and spherical aberration, and with an objective lens between 2½ and 3½ inches in diameter, will provide ample light-gathering power and will yield sharp, clear images. Such a telescope would be particularly useful in studying the surface of the moon or the planets of the solar system. Anything larger would, however, be considerably more expensive than a reflector telescope of comparable mirror size. A refractor telescope with a four-inch or larger objective lens would not only cost several hundred dollars but might prove impractical for other reasons as well. Such a telescope would be large, long, and bulky; it would be too clumsy for portability and would require a permanent mounting. What is more, unless you live high in the mountains where the air is clear, or on the desert far from smoggy cities, you might actually not be able to see much more with a large (four-inch or larger lens) refractor telescope than with a smaller one, since dirt and dust in the air and interfering sky glow might cancel out any advantage of greater light-gathering power and magnification.

For a beginner, a modestly priced refractor telescope with an objective lens ranging from $2\frac{1}{2}$ to $3\frac{1}{2}$ inches will serve admirably well until you become experienced enough in its use to determine what improvements you need for the kind of observing you wish to do. Such an instrument would be light, compact, and portable. It is easy to use, requiring no adjustment of lenses or mirrors, and because it is sealed against dust, dirt, and moisture, it is easy to maintain in good working condition, requiring little more than a clean, dry place for storage and inexpensive lens caps to cover the objective and ocular lenses when the instrument is not in use. Finally, the refractor telescope will provide a bright, clear image of the objects being viewed, and the lenses will never deteriorate if the telescope is properly cared for.

Why, then, do so many amateur astronomers own and use reflector telescopes? Not the least consideration is the matter of cost. Whereas a good refractor telescope with a 3- or $3\frac{1}{2}$-inch objective lens may require a basic investment of $200 or more, highly serviceable reflector telescopes with 3-inch objective mirrors can be obtained new for as little as $50, and those with mirrors ranging from $4\frac{1}{2}$ to 6 inches in diameter may be purchased in the range of $100 to $150 — little more than the cost of a good ten-speed bicycle. Thus for the same price, the amateur astronomer can obtain a telescope with considerably greater light-gathering and resolving power in a reflector telescope than in a refractor one, even though the optical system may not be as fine.

There are, however, some disadvantages. The reflector telescope is open-ended, so that the mirror is subject to the collection of dust, dirt, or moisture. The mirrors of reflector telescopes can get out of adjustment and require periodic correction; they may also have to be resilvered or realuminized from time to time to preserve their reflectivity. In addition, reflector telescopes are somewhat more bulky and difficult to use than refractor telescopes.

These difficulties, however, can be overcome with a minimum amount of experience in using the telescope, and a good reflector telescope with a mirror ranging from 4 to 6 inches will prove to be a thoroughly serviceable instrument.

By far the most common reflector telescopes in amateur use are those of the Newtonian design, in which the reflected image from the mirror is transmitted at a 90-degree angle to the eyepiece on the side of the tube by a flat diagonal mirror suspended near the upper end of the tube. Another common design for reflector telescopes involves the so-called Cassegrainian system of mirrors invented by a French physician, N. Cassegrain (see Fig. 29). In

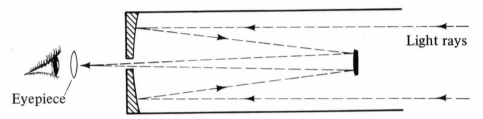

Fig. 29: A modified reflector telescope, Cassegrainian system.

a Cassegrainian telescope, the light waves are reflected from the main objective mirror up to a small convex mirror that is suspended in the telescope's tube. This mirror reflects the light waves back through a small opening in the middle of the large mirror in order to bring them to focus near the eyepiece. Cassegrainian telescopes can be built with much shorter tubes than Newtonian instruments, and are therefore subject to less vibration from wind or ground tremor, but because the Cassegrainian telescope requires two carefully ground and polished mirrors rather than just one, these instruments are correspondingly more expensive, and many of those in amateur use are homemade.

What about making your own telescope? Many experienced amateur astronomers have done so, and in fact this is a major reason why reflector telescopes are as popular as they are among amateurs: they are comparatively easy to make. Ground, polished, and aluminized mirrors can be purchased ready-made from optical supply houses or scientific instrument companies and mounted in a homemade telescope tube with comparatively little effort. It is even possible to grind and polish your own mirror from a glass blank, a less expensive but far more time-consuming procedure. Although it is impossible here to detail the procedure for grinding mirrors or building telescopes, the interested reader will find a wide variety of carefully detailed books on these subjects available in any large public library.

A word of caution is in order, however. Grinding the mirror for a reflector telescope and constructing the telescope to hold it are not excessively complicated, but they do require a great deal of time, patience, and craftsmanship. It is an extremely painstaking task and the pains *must* be taken or a totally useless instrument will result. Before a beginner embarks upon a telescope-building project, he should first secure the counsel and, if possible, the active assistance of someone who has actually built a telescope and understands the procedure thoroughly.

Where can you find such help? It may not be as difficult as it seems. Many high schools have astronomy clubs, and many such clubs have ongoing telescope construction projects. In addition, amateur astronomical societies are organized in many communities throughout the country. These organizations are made up of amateur astronomers from all walks of life with varying degrees of experience in telescope use and telescope building. Some exceptionally fine telescopes have been built either by individual members of such organizations or through the cooperative efforts of members. Six-inch reflecting telescopes are perhaps the most common size for the novice to attempt to build, but expert amateurs have successfully ground, polished, and mounted 12-inch, 16-inch, or even larger mirrors. Refractor telescopes have also been built by amateurs, but for these the complex lens systems must be purchased.

For the beginning amateur, the best course is probably to purchase a small telescope, whether a refractor or a reflector, and learn to use it to the limits of its capacity. As your interest in your hobby grows, and as you gain in knowledge and experience, you will better be able to evaluate for yourself the advantages and disadvantages of attempting to build a telescope.

● *Telescope Footings and Mountings*
Obviously your enjoyment of telescopic observation will depend greatly upon having a well-constructed telescope with good lenses

or a good mirror system. What is not so obvious is that an excellent telescope may be virtually useless unless it is properly mounted and supported for comfortable and efficient use. Your telescope must be mounted on a solid footing which will eliminate jiggling and vibration while the telescope is being used. Without a solid footing, the slightest breeze stirring the air will cause vibration of the instrument, with the result that the object that you are observing will dance madly across the field of vision, rendering observation impossible.

By far the best kind of telescope footing is a solid and sturdy tripod base such as the one illustrated in Figure 30. You can build such a mount for any small telescope with a round block of wood

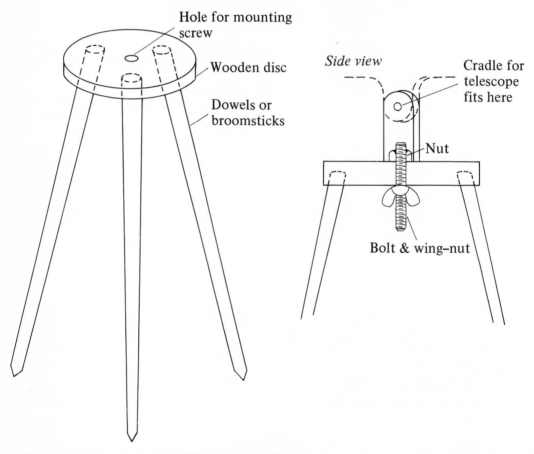

Fig. 30: A homemade tripod telescope footing.

and three broom handles. Figure 31 shows an even more solid three-legged mount for a telescope, also easy to construct, with the additional advantage that you can use it as the base for an equa-

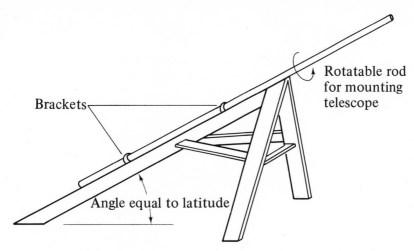

Fig. 31: A solid three-legged telescope mount.

torial mounting for the telescope (see above). A metal camera tripod may be suitable for mounting a small, light telescope, but might prove too shaky for a heavier instrument. Whatever tripod footing you decide upon, whether it be purchased or homemade, test its stability by placing it solidly on the ground or floor, bearing down on the top of it with your hand and twisting at the same time. If the legs tend to turn with this twisting motion, the tripod is probably too flimsy to be useful and a heavier-duty rig should be obtained or constructed.

Once you have a solid tripod footing, you will then need an adjustable mounting to secure the telescope itself to the footing. Obviously it is not possible to sight the telescope on a celestial object, fix it firmly in position, and then proceed to observe indefinitely. Because of the Earth's continuous rotation on its axis, the stars and other celestial objects appear to have a continuous motion across the sky in a great circle around the axis of the north celestial pole. When observing with the unaided eye, you see this motion of the stars as a very slow arc with only the polestar remaining in almost precisely the same position in the sky from one hour to the next. But with the magnification of a telescope, this motion of the stars in the sky means that many objects will very quickly move out of the field of view if the telescope is held in a fixed position.

Thus any mounting you use to secure your telescope to its tripod footing must be easily and smoothly adjustable so that you can constantly move the telescope to "track" or follow the object you are studying. There are two common types of telescope mountings that can accomplish this goal. The simplest, illustrated in Figure

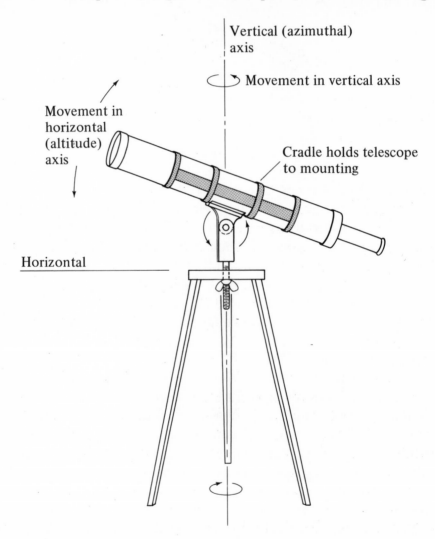

Fig. 32: Telescope with altazimuth mounting.

32, will allow you to move the telescope smoothly and gently in either one or both of two separate *axes of rotation*: an up-and-down or vertical axis, so that the telescope can be moved from the horizon straight up across the sky to the zenith, the so-called "altitude" axis; and a horizontal or "azimuth" axis to permit the telescope to be moved from side to side across the sky. This kind of mounting, which really involves a sort of universal joint to permit adjustment of the telescope, is called an *altazimuth mount*.

Such an arrangement, simple as it is, has one serious disadvantage. In order to track and observe a given star for any period of time, you must make frequent adjustment of the telescope's position in both the horizontal and vertical directions. Very inexpensive commercial altazimuth mounts are often made with a ball-and-socket clamp or a system of rotating rods and turnscrews which may be very difficult to keep in adjustment. Better-made (and correspondingly more expensive) altazimuth mounts are equipped with fine-adjustment knobs that will allow very slight movement of the telescope in each axis of rotation and make it possible for you to follow a given object in the sky quite skillfully with a little practice.

A homemade altazimuth mount must be carefully built and well lubricated in order to allow smooth movement of the telescope without jarring its position. A very tiny accidental movement of the telescope will often remove the object you are observing completely from the telescopic field so that you will have to search to find it again, a procedure that can be very tedious. If you plan to use an altazimuth mount, or if you purchase a telescope equipped with one, see that it is well lubricated and then plan to spend some time learning to move the telescope slowly and smoothly throughout its entire range of motion in both axes so that, when you are actually star watching, you will be able to make the necessary adjustments almost automatically without accidental jarring or jolting.

One of the major disadvantages of the altazimuth mount — the need for two separate position adjustments — can be avoided by equipping your telescope with a somewhat more complicated mounting, the so-called *equatorial mount*. As we have seen, the apparent motion of the stars in the sky is in an arc centering around the north celestial pole. If one axis of your telescope's orientation can be pointed and fixed directly on the polestar — the one point in the sky that does not seem to move — then any object in the telescope's field of vision can be followed with just one adjustment to move the telescope in the same arc that the stars appear to be following.

To achieve this orientation for your telescope, it is necessary to make the main supporting axis of the telescope a rotating bar which can be secured to the solid footing in such a way that it is pointing directly at the polestar from wherever you are observing. One way to accomplish this is to construct an angulated three-legged footing, as illustrated in Figure 33, with the long leg built at precisely the same angle to the ground as the angle of latitude

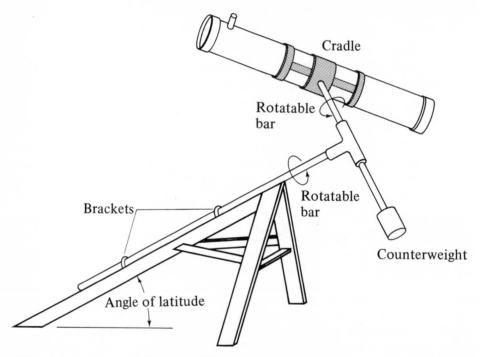

Fig. 33: Telescope with equatorial mounting.

of your location. The angle can be determined by checking in any atlas to find the number of degrees north latitude at which your home or backyard observatory is located. This angle will vary anywhere from 35 degrees in New Mexico to 40 degrees in New Jersey, or 47 degrees in Washington State. A revolving rod can then be attached along the length of this leg of the footing and extended beyond for mounting the telescope. Once the footing has been oriented so that the rod points directly at the North Star, the telescope mounted on the rod can be pointed at any star in the sky and will then require only the lateral or sideways adjustment to remain fixed on that object as it moves in its great arc around the celestial pole.

You can easily confirm that you have achieved the proper angle and alignment of the rod for your equatorial mount simply by focusing the mounted telescope on the North Star. If the alignment is correct, this star should remain in the telescope's field for prolonged periods without any adjustment at all. Once you have determined the proper position and alignment for the mounting rod and the footing that supports it, mark the position of the footing for future reference by means of mounting pegs driven into the ground, or build a small permanent mounting platform with marks to indicate the proper position of the footing. This way the equatorial mount can be returned to the proper alignment time after time without requiring new adjustment each time.

With an equatorial mount, you will be able to study celestial objects for prolonged periods with only a single adjustment of the telescope to keep the object within the field of vision. It is even possible to purchase an inexpensive mechanical clock drive to make this adjustment for you so that you will have to pay little or no attention to adjustment while observing. An equatorial mount is decidedly worth the effort to build if you have an established place from which you will do your observing night after night, or if you intend to use your telescope for astronomical photography, since any photographs made through a telescope will require prolonged time exposures and the object you are photographing must be held at the same point in the telescope's field of vision for several minutes if a clear photograph is to be possible.

In viewing the moon or the planets, which have a discernible motion in the sky independent of either the Earth's rotation or the apparent motion of the stars, it will be necessary to make additional altazimuthal adjustments to the telescope even with an equatorial mount, but these adjustments will be minor compared to those that would be necessary without the equatorial feature.

● *Accessories for Your Telescope*

In addition to your telescope, its mounting, and the supportive footing, there are a few accessories that will help make your telescopic observation more simple, comfortable, and pleasurable. Most important, perhaps, is a *sighting scope* attached to the tube of your telescope to help you locate the celestial object you want to observe. The magnified field of vision of your telescope, large as it may appear in the eyepiece, actually represents only a very tiny patch of sky. If you were to use the telescope itself to search for a given celestial object you wanted to observe, you would spend enormous amounts of time and often fail to find the object even at that.

The sighting scope is nothing more than a small, low-power spyglass which is bolted to the side of the telescope in perfect alignment with the telescope's optical system. When you have decided what you want to observe with the telescope, the sighting scope can be used to find it in the sky so that the telescope adjustment can be fixed at this point. If the sighting scope is in proper alignment, and if you center the desired object within its field of vision, the object should also be within the field of vision of the telescope itself, or so nearby that it can be found with a minimum of searching.

If you have a refracting telescope, or a Cassegrainian reflector with the eyepiece mounted in line with the telescope tube, you may find a so-called *star diagonal prism* useful. This is simply a device that bends the light coming through the eyepiece at 90 degrees to the telescope tube so that the viewer can, in effect, look sideways toward the telescope rather than up the length of it for convenient viewing, as illustrated in Figure 34.

If you have a good telescope, you will also want at least some choice of eyepieces or ocular lenses to use for different magnifications. Most telescope eyepieces are standardized to $1\frac{1}{4}$ inches in diameter, but eyepieces of different focal length — and usually of different lens construction — can provide low-power, medium-power, or high-power magnification.

Many inexperienced amateurs assume, when first using a telescope, that the instrument will be the more useful the higher the magnifying power. But with experience you will find that this is

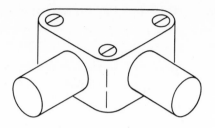

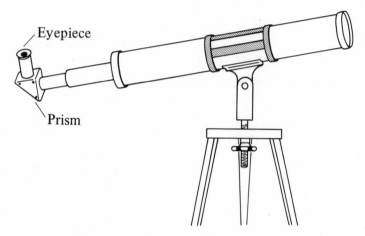

Fig. 34: A star diagonal prism.

not necessarily so. There are many celestial objects for study which are far better observed under a low power than under higher magnification. In studying the surface of the moon, for example, you will find that a low- or medium-power eyepiece will enable you to see a large segment of the moon's surface at once in a single field of vision, whereas with a higher magnification you would only be able to see a small segment of the moon's surface and would lose much of the three-dimensional quality of the view. Also, the higher the magnification the more swiftly a given object "drifts" out of the telescopic field, so that the lower the magnification you are using the less adjustment of the telescope's position will be necessary as you continue your observation.

A variety of special corrective lenses are also available as attachments to the eyepiece or ocular lens for special purposes. The so-called Barlow lens, for example, which can be attached ahead of the eyepiece, can double or triple the magnifying power of the lens that is in use. Another kind of modifying lens is useful if you wish to use your telescope for viewing objects on the ground as well as in the sky. This is a so-called *image erector* lens which can be placed ahead of the eyepiece lens to reinvert the upside-down image that you would otherwise see through the telescope. Such a modifying lens is of no value for astronomical viewing, however, since it reduces the amount of light coming through your telescope, and the reinversion of the image of celestial objects is of no advantage whatever in observing them.

Finally, if you are interested in experimenting with astronomical photography, you will have to obtain a camera adapter to fit onto the eyepiece of your telescope in order to attach and support the camera for long time exposures. For any kind of satisfactory astronomical photography you will need a 35-mm. camera with an excellent lens and a choice of film qualities and speeds. You will also need an equatorial mount for your telescope with a mechanical drive to keep a given celestial object precisely located in the telescopic field long enough for time exposures to be made. Standard eyepiece adapters for 35-mm. cameras are available from scientific equipment companies or camera shops.

● *Purchasing a Telescope*

Even a comparatively small telescope will involve a significant investment, and you will want to be as certain as possible that the instrument you are selecting will really meet your needs. Thus you should devote as much time and care to shopping for a telescope as you would in purchasing a bicycle, a camera, or a stereo set. Small commercially manufactured telescopes, whether refractors or reflectors, are available in a wide variety of sizes and qualities with an even wider variety of refinements, and you should familiarize yourself thoroughly with what is available at what cost before you make a final selection.

If you live in or near a large metropolitan area, you can begin your search with the Yellow Pages of the telephone directory under "Telescopes" and make a list of the business places — scientific instrument stores, camera shops, optical shops, or even hobby shops — that carry a stock of telescopes. Then visit these stores, examine the telescopes available, collect literature about their qualities and properties, compare prices, and if possible discuss the instruments you find interesting with others who are more experienced in amateur astronomy. Consider not only the telescopes themselves, but also the footings and mountings that are available, the types and powers of eyepieces, the sighting scopes, the adjustment mechanisms, and any other refinements that are offered. Check the pages of popular science magazines such as *Sky and Telescope* or *Natural History* for the advertisements of reputable companies that make, sell, and distribute telescopes; many such companies will provide free catalogs and other detailed information about various types of telescopes they handle. Only when you are thoroughly acquainted with the wide variety of choice that exists, and have carefully considered all factors including type of telescope, size, quality, and cost, should you make a final decision. And, finally, when you have settled on a telescope and purchased it, familiarize yourself thoroughly with the operating instructions and check the nature of the warranty or guarantee so that you understand clearly what to do if the instrument should fail to function as you expect it to.

What about buying a used telescope? Such instruments are frequently offered for sale in the classified sections of large-city newspapers and it is quite possible to obtain a good used telescope for a much lower price than you would have to pay for a comparable instrument purchased new. Special caution must be exercised, however, since it is always possible that a used telescope is being offered for sale because it no longer functions properly. In considering any used telescope, arrange to take the instrument for a period of time on approval before you are committed to buy it, and utilize that time to test its function or have it checked over carefully by some experienced person before you make a final decision.

Whatever your choice, bear in mind that a small and inexpensive instrument may be the best possible selection for your first telescope. Not only can you gain much enjoyment from learning to use it properly, but you will also be discovering its limitations and disadvantages and can use this firsthand experience — the best counsel of all — later when you seek to buy or build a larger and better instrument.

● *Exploring the Sky by Telescope*
With a small but serviceable telescope, your exploration of the heavens will take on a totally new and exciting dimension, for the telescope will extend your viewing horizons immeasurably. Not only will you rediscover familiar objects in a new richness of detail, but also many other celestial objects will now be observable for the first time. Whole books have been written for the amateur astronomer about telescopic exploration of the heavens; here it is only possible to hint at some of the new horizons a telescope can reveal.

Within our solar system many old friends will be observable now in far greater clarity and detail than ever before. Much as you can learn by studying the surface of the moon with binoculars, a telescopic study will prove infinitely more rewarding; once you have learned the major landmarks, the telescope will bring even minor surface details into sharp focus. The planets, too, will prove far more exciting to study. For the first time you will be able to distinguish the magnificent ring system of Saturn. Titan, the largest of Saturn's moons, can also be identified. As for mighty Jupiter, even a small telescope will resolve the four major satellites clearly, and you will be able to follow their progress in their orbits around the planet. What is more, during a favorable opposition, you will be able to see the planetary disk so clearly that the surface markings become apparent. You will discover that Jupiter can be observed with the telescope not only at night, but also often during daylight hours as well, and that it presents a quite startlingly different appearance during daylight observation than at night.

Venus, too, can be studied in daylight as well as in darkness. Mars will present more difficulty; nighttime viewing will be necessary, and its surface markings are seldom clear even with a powerful telescope. But with patience you, like other astronomers before you, will come upon those occasional periods of exceptional visual clarity in which the mysterious fuzziness of this planet seems to clear, at least for a few moments; the polar cap will suddenly stand out startlingly white in contrast to the orange-yellow planetary surface, and the strange blue-gray mottling of that surface will come into clear and unmistakable focus. It is at times like these that Mars will cease to be a mere tiny disk in the sky, and you will see it, at least momentarily, as it really is: another world as varied and unique as our own, similar to our Earth in as many ways as it is different, an alien world that man has already begun to explore by remote control and will inevitably one day explore in person.

Probably no one alive today will be on hand to witness the first meaningful exploration of star systems beyond our own Sun; the distances are too great, and the necessary technology still too far removed. But with a telescope you will be able to retrace the steps of astronomical explorers throughout the ages who have already learned vast amounts about the universe of our galaxy and other distant galaxies. Stellar objects you were able to see only indistinctly with binoculars — the great nebula in Orion, the splendid globular cluster in Hercules, the great spiral galaxy in Andromeda, to name but a few — stand forth in exciting detail in the telescopic field.

Such great luminous clouds of gas as the North American Nebula that lies just below Deneb in the constellation Cygnus, the Swan, will be easily visible. So will the famous Horsehead Nebula just above the first star of Orion's belt. You will be able to locate and distinguish the double star cluster in the constellation Perseus, or the strange "demon star" Algol, a binary star system in which the small, bright member of the pair of stars is periodically eclipsed by its much larger and dimmer partner so that the star's brightness suddenly dims by as much as two-thirds regularly every seventy hours. You will be able to observe such famous "smoke rings in the sky" as the beautiful Ring Nebula in the constellation Lyra — an enormous cloud of gas surrounding a very faint but hot star which can barely be distinguished itself but which nevertheless illuminates the gas cloud with its radiation.

With further telescopic exploration, you will see for yourself how many of the stars with which you have previously become familiar are in fact true double or binary stars. Castor, for example, one of the "heavenly twins" of Gemini, is in fact a binary star with one of the pair of stars approximately 2½ times as bright as the other. Rigel, the brilliant blue-white star marking Orion's foot, is another binary that you will be able to distinguish with your telescope.

There is literally no end to the celestial objects you can learn to identify in your telescopic exploration of the heavens. But just observing will not be enough; the more you see, the more you will want to learn, so that your hobby will lead you inevitably to reading as well as observing. You will become familiar with detailed star maps, atlases, and observers' guides, testing your skill at finding and observing unusual stellar objects that you will find listed. You will become acquainted with the strange story of Charles Messier, the devoted comet hunter of the eighteenth century who, in searching the skies for new comets, became so annoyed by the variety of uncharted stellar objects that he found — clusters of stars, for example, or a variety of fuzzy or hazy patches in the sky — that he finally drew up a catalog of over a hundred of these objects as reminders to himself of "things to be avoided." Today Messier's comets are all but forgotten, yet the stellar objects listed in Messier's famous catalog now constitute a standard list of star clusters and nebulae available to the amateur observer, even including distant galaxies.

You will also become acquainted with this catalog and learn to identify a great many of the objects listed there which were, to their discoverer, a mere nuisance — such objects as the famous Crab Nebula in the constellation Taurus, the Lagoon Nebula in Sagittarius, the Trifid Nebula, also in Sagittarius; the Owl Nebula in Ursa Major; or the "Sombrero Hat," a spiral galaxy in the constellation Virgo. Further reading will lead you on to still more new discoveries, and you will find that the amount you can learn will be limited only by the amount of time and effort you wish to invest.

Backyard astronomy can, in fact, evolve into a fascinating and engrossing lifelong hobby. For those who become deeply interested, there is virtually no limit to the enjoyment that is possible. You can share in that enjoyment whether you are a casual observer whiling away a few minutes or hours on occasional evenings, learning to identify the constellations and peering at the moon's surface through binoculars, or whether you go on to become deeply engrossed in the study of astronomy, outfitting your own observatory with an effective telescope, communicating with others who share your interest, and studying as well as observing. For the casual observer as well as the serious amateur astronomer, backyard astronomy is a simple introduction to a fascinating world of knowledge, and no matter how deeply you choose to become involved, it is not likely that you will ever find it boring.

ADDITIONAL
READING

Danhour, Robert E. *Telescopes for the Amateur Astronomer.* New Augusta, Ind.: Editors and Engineers Ltd., 1966.

Fermi, Laura and Bernardini, Gilbert. *Galileo and the Scientific Revolution.* New York: Basic Books, 1961.

Menzel, Donald H. *Astronomy.* New York: Random House, 1970.

Moore, Patrick. *Amateur Astronomy.* New York: W. W. Norton Co., 1968.

————. *The Atlas of The Universe.* Chicago: Rand McNally, 1970.

Muirden, James. *Stars and Planets.* New York: Thomas Y. Crowell Co., 1965.

Nourse, Alan E. *Nine Planets* (revised edition). New York: Harper & Row, 1970.

————. *Venus and Mercury.* New York: Franklin Watts, 1972.

Rogers, Frances. *5000 Years of Stargazing.* Philadelphia: Lippincott, 1964.

Wilkins, H. Percy and Moore, Patrick. *Making and Using a Telescope.* London: Eyre & Spottiswoode, 1959.

INDEX

ABOUT
THE
AUTHOR

Alan E. Nourse is one of America's
best-known writers on astronomical subjects for
young people. He is the author of *Nine Planets*
and several works of science fiction.
A former practicing physician, Dr. Nourse
makes his home in North Bend, Washington.
His latest book for Franklin Watts, Inc.
is *Venus and Mercury* (a First Book).